BROKEN ROAD TO BADASS

RELEASE THE PAIN & STAND IN YOUR POWER

TINA FRALEY

eGenCo

eGenCo

Chambersburg, Pennsylvania

Email: info@egen.co

Website: www.egen.co

facebook.com/egenbooks

youtube.com/egenpub

pinterest.com/eGenDMP

instagram.com/egen.co

Cover design by Kristen Laidig

Cover photography by Stephanie Patterson

Interior layout by Kevin Lepp

Library of Congress Cataloging-in-Publication Data

Library of Congress Control Number: 2021906552

ISBN: 978-1-68019-020-5   Paperback
          978-1-68019-021-2   eBook

TABLE OF CONTENTS

FOREWORD

Trauma is a powerful drug. Not unlike heroin or cocaine, its experience has the capacity to alter one's mind, emotions, and physical being. Trauma can come in all shapes and sizes and linger in every-day-life. Trauma can show up instantaneously and without warning. It is rare that someone has never experienced ANY trauma.

The manner in which we work through, around, and within trauma in our lives is personal and individualistic; an event—ANY event, really—can cause trauma which can wreak havoc for us, our families, friends, professional networks, and anyone else with whom we interact.

Bottom line: Trauma sucks. But for every negative, the law of opposites tells us there is a positive. In no way does that mean that trauma creates positivity—no, trauma is hard, debilitating, horrific, and at times it can feel all-powering and soul-crushing. The ability to fight through and around trauma is what this book is about— the resilience of the will to live a better life by creating a pathway from which we may see ourselves traveling.

The journey you are about to begin may allow you to make incredible sense of your life's pathway and chose the vessel to wade through your complicated circumstances in life. Even so, it is important to note that there is never a time that we may be clear of all trauma. Where we can shine, though, is our ability to work through it all, using the tools, gifts, and power we know we have, but sometimes, cannot reach. For Tina Fraley—and possibly you—it is the sharing of her story about wading through the ocean of trauma and finding herself in all her power that may lead us to look for a similar pathway. A path that provides the healing and compassionate self-empowerment we crave to navigate the murky waters of life.

We must view ourselves as complicated and worthy, strong and vulnerable, and striving for doing great things with a complete understanding that failure is OK if we learn from it. That's badassery; the key to the fight when trauma has its hand on your back screaming, "You will not prevail" is your ability to stand up and shout back, "Watch me work."

Tina's personal and deeply vulnerable story helps her lay the foundation for us in any way we can use it; her empowerment creates the opportunity for our own badassery to come out and shine. This book can be triggering for many, and for most folks, it can be difficult to read. By taking the journey down Tina's pathway of her empowerment and awakening to her own strength, we might just learn a bit about getting up from the darkest places to achieve the greatest things in our lives, honoring the badassery we all have, and willing it to the surface to thrive.

Andi Overton
Director of Recruiting, John Hopkins University's Carey School of Business
Board member of Woman to Woman Mentoring
Co-host of the television show "The Flip Side"

ACKNOWLEDGMENTS

My Love, thank you for standing in the sun with me and being a grain of sand. Thank you for your patience, your laughter, and letting me just curl up and listen to your heartbeat. Thank you so much for saying "YES" with me! I love you immensely. God blessed the broken road that led me straight to you...

Zach, Hart, Nikki, Justin, Serenity, Mason, and Bella, you have inspired me to grow and learn to live an adventure in every moment of my life. It is my greatest joy to witness each of you grow beyond my dreams and into your own. You are all extraordinary, and I am so grateful to be your Mom.

There are many, many friends whose hearts and hands helped bind this book and build my dream of publishing it. Thank you to my mountain-climbing friends and all the high achievers I have been blessed to learn from for literally taking me to new heights and capturing the moments with me. Thank you to my coffee-house crew for listening to every Divine download. Thank you to every member of the Your Power House Community. Thank you to my editor and my publishing team for taking a chance with me and helping me continue to rise.

To every reader, you are worth it all and you always will be.

Thank you. I am sorry. Please forgive me. I love you.
– Ho'oponopono

INTRODUCTION

Let's clear things up from the jump. You are not broken. You have never been broken. You will never be broken. You are an extraordinary human being physically living the incredibly emotional adventure we all call life. You are on the broken road to Badass right now and that can be hard. It can be overwhelming and frustrating. It can also be exhilarating and inspiring. Either way you are the one responsible for all of it. It's *your* joy, *your* pain, *your* hurt, *your* healing. And until you own that truth you are lying in areas of your mind and heart that need your full attention. Here is where you decide to call BS on all the things you come across that it turns out you don't actually believe anymore, or maybe never even did but just kept on carrying the family torch of dis-ease.

The fact of the matter is that you can't heal someone else any more than someone else can heal you. And yet how many of us spend entire lifetimes trying to make things better for others before we focus that same attention on ourselves? We are going to stop that insanity right here, right now. For the next 100-plus pages I really want you to be selfish. Squirrel away some time that you can read this and really give your attention to it so the take-aways you will have can be immediately implemented.

Alright, here we go. You are about to witness what I now fondly call Project Pinocchio. What in the world does a marionette have to do with any of this? Well, there's definitely no-strings-attached to living your authentic life. However, there are some long-lasting repercussions when we choose not to. Remember what happened to Pinocchio's nose? Good! Then you will also remember how he kept it from happening over and over again. Wouldn't life be so much easier if we could just sit back and watch it all unfold, fall apart, and come perfectly back together again, all within a Walt-Disney hour? Yes, but how much would be missing? How many real moments in life do we miss because we are caught up in keeping up the lies we tell ourselves? You don't lie? You do. And so did I.

It takes patience and compassion to be who you have never been before. True transparency is required to self-explore and live authentically in your purpose. I won't lie to you now, my friends. It's not easy at first. It gets downright ugly. But I am here to attest to the fact that every step along the way is worth it. That *you* are worth it. And the people you love most in this world are worth the steps you are about to take on the journey to figuring it out. I've had many tipping points in my life over the last 40+ years with the scales, both literally and figuratively, that landed me with one of life's greatest ultimatums: Live this life right now while you are still here to do so.

I'm going to walk you through my story in the hopes that you will find the comfort and courage to finally live your life. My experiences have all added up to this crazy-amazing moment where I am sitting here at a beach-side table, bribing myself with coffee and sandy walks, typing this in complete awe of how it all finally came to be. I'm visualizing each one of you extraordinary badasses being able to read this and reframe your lives because you are holding a piece of proof (or listening if I pulled off a contract with Audible), that shows you how to rise up and release the lies because one woman shared why and how she did it and came out the other side.

I've been writing this story my entire life. I didn't take over the rights to it until my seventh child was born though, almost nine years ago now. Yes, I have seven incredible little lives that will forever call me "Mom". Each one of them has helped me to see things in myself that I had refused to for years. You will get to know my husband and best friend in this life and how I broke his heart by not mending my own. And I'll share the emotional aspects of physically losing over one hundred pounds. All that changes a girl over time as I'm sure you can imagine. I'm positive you are the type of person that understands that there is more to life than just surviving it.

If you are like me at all, there is a huge part of your soul right now ready for lift off. But every time you feel like you are set to go and you take that deep breath in, there is this other part of you that swoops in and fizzles out all your momentum, leaving you with a *why bother?* mentality. Well, I promise not to go all guru on you at any point in this book. But you will be changed by the end for reading it. You will remember that part of you that confidently knows how to say, "Hell, yeah!" You will want to cozy up next to that part of you, plan out your life, and live the best you can every single day.

She's in there, I promise! She may be hiding underneath the dishes, doctor appointments, workload, marital tensions, playdates, practices, laundry, and packed lunches, but that badass is in there! It's time she breaks out and plays. As a trainer and coach that is one of the things I share with each of my newfound friends in fitness and healthy living. Don't worry, I also promise not to throw any burpees at you along the way. I became a trainer years after I figured out how to lose the weight and after going to fifteen years of school for a counseling degree. I realized there was no actual support for those of us still experiencing the emotional aspects of our physical transformations. It turns out that exercising can induce tears and emotional breakdowns that have absolutely nothing to do with jumping, squatting, holding a plank, or isolated curls.

First things first, this is not a quick-fix-your-life book. It is not a book on how to lose pounds on the scale, although I will be sharing that adventure. It is not a how-to-parent-better book, but you will see how that turns out, too (all seven kids are still thriving). It most definitely is not going to give you the seven extraordinary steps to wonderful wifedom as my husband Heath can attest to happily today. And sorry, there's no money-mindset-reboot chapter in here either, but you will notice the abundance growing as you read. That's the coolest part; just like in life, things are not always what you expect, but rather what you intend. So, please acknowledge the disclaimer here, that none of what I am going to share with you is meant to replace professional or medical advice. I also need you to know that there will be memories that I share that may be considered a trigger if you are someone who has ever experienced physical or mental abuse.

In short, this is a book about how I decided to live more of my life while I was still here to do so and why it's imperative to start doing the same right now. It's time to live and be more than the sum of your circumstances. We all wake up at different moments in this journey. We all have a next first step while we are still six feet up. It is not too late to begin again and take that first intentional breath of air deep into your lungs, pulling in all the joy and releasing yourself from everything you no longer want to lie about loving. I hope you are finally willing to open your bags and unpack them. This is the adventure of a lifetime.

CHAPTER 1

BROKEN BOULEVARD

Hi, y'all! I'm Tina, and this is my life's story, unpacked. These experiences are from my (professional & expert) perspective as a woman who survived and is now standing in the sun with her truth. (*Scandal* fans may get that reference.) My goal is to help you unpack and sort through your own baggage and, in the process, talk you through letting go of the lies weighing you down in this life.

So, let's do this. Let's adventure on together. It's time to dance it out and friend-request your authentic self. You get to write the rest of your story, where the extraordinary gift you are shines through completely. I like to think of it like those books we read as kids where we can choose our own adventure. I want you to really think on this next statement because there are going to be many of you that straight-up do not believe it. I used to turn my head at it also, so just know there's a time and a place where it will be your truth. The only things stopping you from living the life you want are the choices you make right now and the lies you maintain daily to prove your choice as true.

I promise we will loop back around to this one, so jot it down, voice-memo it, or screenshot it for later. Right now, I want you to take a deep breath in and slowly release it for a count of 10. How did that feel? Wonky? Weird?

Oddly placed in the beginning of a book? I feel you. When I use breathing exercises, it always feels slightly odd at first. I have struggled with anxiety since I was very young and had my share of coping mechanisms over the years, but I actively share the joy that breathing exercises bring me when I use them. My hope is that when you read the end of that last paragraph and you jotted down that one-two punch in the feels, that it caught your breath just a little.

You see, when I first came across those words, strung together in that ever-so-effective order, my breath caught in my throat. It stopped me in my tracks. I realized in that exact moment that it was all up to me. What I believed and how I perceived my life was up to me. The choices I made were up to me to make. As cliché as it will sound, no matter what I believed, I was going to be right. This gives you a very different perspective to filter your life through. Our perspectives will make or break our lives. Take a moment and think about how you view your life right now. Are you happy with it? Are you living the life you say you want? Do you look for the ways to serve others in kindness and compassion each day? Are you doing the same for yourself? Or are you maintaining a storyline with lies that keeps you disconnected, incongruent, and ineffective in your own life?

I had to ask myself those same questions over and over again. There was no overnight success story. But as we begin this walk together, I want you to start envisioning the warrior inside yourself. Our ability to treat ourselves with the same grace, kindness, and compassion we show others turns out to be the solution to most of our problems when it comes to fully living life. In short, love yourself as much as you love the people around you!

When I started to fully comprehend that little life nugget, this adventure changed completely. I evolved from the wounded walking to the warrior I was in every facet of my life. I will never forget the moment this realization started to grow inside my mind. I was sitting across from Heath who was trying to comfort me through yet another emotional overload, and I saw myself reflected in his glasses. He had no idea of the tidal waves of trauma that I was keeping away from him out of my own fear. Four years into our relationship and four years outside the daily prison I lived in with my oldest five children was still not enough time to track down *normal.* I had to play the part though. In this scene in my life, I was wife. I was mother. I was not the rape victim. I was not the previous prisoner spinning out of control with the newfound freedom and extreme fear of it. As the snot trails rolled down my cheeks and my red eyes flowed with tears that day I was just the girl trying to see it different.

As he held my hand and told me how much he loved me, I battled my own beliefs. He again was trying to help me see who I really am and let me know that he could see how much pain I was in every day. He was trying to reach me. He wiped my tear-matted hair away from my face and tried to console me. In that moment, I remember asking myself, "How can this man love such a mess so much"? I remember the first time I asked him that question straight to his face as I sat on the bottom stair in his townhouse on Quailbridge. The house that would bring us full circle years later as we rented the home directly across from it, making it our front-yard reminder of a past unprocessed. The wounded walking warrior I was then looked love in the face and diplomatically, callously, explained exactly why he did not want to take on me and five kids. That time on the stairs, he was the one that interrupted that default BS story I was spewing as he reached out his hand and pulled me into his arms promising, "I got you, all of you". In front of him those four years out of hell, it was me emotionally standing up and allowing that internal inquisition the opportunity to call out my own BS story.

There were no doubts when it came to Heath, I trusted him. I loved him. I enjoyed him. I enjoyed myself with him. What's more than all of that was that I fully appreciated and recognized who I was in way I had forgotten since we last had known one another as kids. I chose him to live my life with me, to help raise my kids. In reminding myself of that truth, I found a BS lie I was spinning inside myself that needed to be released.

Uncover the lie: If the amazing man you love, that you were raising little lives with, co-creating an entire new life with, looked at you with all that love and pride and joy, and you don't believe you're worth it, girl, it's time to check yourself. He was one of your choices! The real question for me wasn't whether or not I was worthy of love, or his love, or anything else. The real question was whether or not I trusted myself to make positive, healthy, compassionate, and loving choices in my own life. The truth today is that I am capable of making these choices, and I made them. The lie I was maintaining was that I was

4

completely incapable and utterly unworthy of anything positive, healthy, or what I deemed as normal.

Uncovering the lie is only the first step in this adventure. Unpacking it is another. Feeling it all and letting it hurt one last time follows that step. And then there is releasing the lie and surrendering to the opportunity it was for you. The final step is radical gratitude. In the effort to be completely transparent with you, I am totally with you if you are reading this and arriving at a WTF moment. If there is a part of you that is screaming inside at the very thought of being *grateful* for trauma or any sideways sequences in your life. Trust me, I get it and I can hear you loud and clear.

I tapped into that primal scream too, the one that seems to lay dormant just below the surface of who we show up as every day. Truth and gratitude go hand-in-hand, though. This life is meant to be lived. Truth? We can't live out of a place full of lack and lies. Truth? We have a right, a privilege, and a responsibility to dig deep and *uncover* the things preventing us from fully engaging. Truth? Are you doing that? Are you living your truth or maintaining your lies?

Did you wake up today grateful for that first purposeful inhale or simply arrive at yet another day in doldrum land? Did you squint your eyes and smile as you curled up to your loved one? Or blankly stare at their sleeping face, talking yourself out of the opportunity to enjoy one another before the kids and life come knocking on the door? Did you feel the floor beneath your feet as you stood and stretched? Or did you grumble your way up and out,

5

shuffling your feet across the room and straight into your routine? Did you even notice how strong your heartbeat was and how effortlessly it was keeping your body alive?

If none of that took place and every day is just a day to you, I want to tell you a universal truth. You can choose to believe me or not. My guess is that you are already on the side of believing or you would have retired your reading around the breathing exercise paragraph. Friend, there's more. There is so much more truth in this life, to who you are, to who you are becoming, and the toughest truth, who you have been and refused to own along the way. This adventure we call life has been giving you the opportunity to see and be radically grateful this whole time.

You may have some lies to uncover, unpack, experience one more time, release, and have radical gratitude for right now. Let that shit stop running your life and dictating who you really are to the core. This broken road home leads to the badass that made it this far and now the rest of your story is up to you. And I totally get it. This sounds extreme. It sounds daunting. And in some ways, it may seem impossible.

I liked my lies for a very long time, too. They were who I was and how I understood the world for almost thirty-three years. That filter doesn't have to be applied a second longer than you choose it. That's crazy to even think about, let alone acknowledge. Who would want to take this purposeful road down Broken Boulevard? Who willingly acknowledges they are the wounded walking? *You do*! You are the one who has the power, the time, and the tenacity to comb back through this life and look for all the lies that kept the BS train running at full-speed, hurting everyone in its path, including you.

Let's look at this from a very logical and pragmatic vantage point. Those lies worked and served a purpose! Or we wouldn't have lied. There was some kind of beneficial, deemed worthy, relative ROI for maintaining the lies. Like a child who steals the cookie out of the jar, the cookie was wanted, desired, and enjoyed right up until there was consequence, ramification, or discipline. My lies, even though they went down just as easily as the cookies over the years, served a very specific purpose. They held me up, kept me safe, and allowed me to vicariously experience everything I believed I couldn't do. My Famous Amos cookies weren't pulling that off, although they did become a comfort-mechanism along the way.

The truth is, lies need more lies. They support themselves. They don't question truths. They seek only confirmation and proof to sustain themselves. My lies made me feel safe and comfortable in a world I was terrified to be in. My lies kept me in a self-imposed prison and consequently imprisoned my children and the very man who tried to help us. I will venture to say that your lies keep you safe and comfortable but are imprisoning you and yours to a life sentence of denial and survival.

Another way to look at those lies is to consider them your limiting beliefs. For our purposes here, we are going to just call BS on the hyperbole. A lie is a lie is a lie. There are several pivotal lies that I have found on my path towards standing in the sun again. I want to take you to the most recent one I discovered as it helped me see what I had to do moving forward.

I was on my way back from a conference held in Phoenix, Arizona. I was ecstatic to be spending five days away from my Maryland winter. I had come to the astounding realization that my lies kept me from living my life. It had been a complete act of God that I was even at that conference to begin with, so I knew there was most definitely something for me to uncover this time. The previous three years had been a concentrated focus on reclaiming who I was. Often that looked like a stumbling, blubbering, hot mess express. I was growing more compassionate with myself and discovering that no one has their shit together as much as I assumed they did. I most certainly did not have my shit together, and that was OK.

Remember where I mentioned that you have to be willing to grow into who you are? Well, my friends, if you are lying your ass off about who that is, you can't grow. Where there is no growth, there is no life. By its own definition, life is "the condition that distinguishes animals and plants from inorganic matter, including the capacity for growth and continual change preceding death."[1] My decision to stop being what the good folks at Oxford would define as inorganic matter was pretty pivotal, as it turned out. In other words, let's stop being lumps on a log, join the living, and grow! That sounds fairly innocuous, right?

So, there I was, on my way back from Phoenix for

---

1   *Oxford U.S. English Dictionary, s.v.* "life," by Oxford University Press, accessed January 4, 2021, https://www.lexico.com/en/definition/life.

the 3rd time. I had been attending self-development conferences and actively pursuing my own growth for a few years now, but this one wasn't like any of the others. I went solely and completely for me, by myself, with a new calm, core-deep knowing, that I was fully present, ready to receive, and willing to grow.

The weather was not flight-friendly that day at all. I am not a fan of flying to begin with, but on days with storm clouds and wind-related delays it's definitely not my jam! I broke out my breathing techniques and a meditation mantra in my brain that evening. "Release, release, release, releeeeeeeeaaaasssssseeee, etc." It wasn't working. I was breaking a damn sweat trying to release. I was also trying to get any one of my three devices to just pull up the Netflix movie I had downloaded so I could distract my brain, and not a one of them would work. That left me with two options (or so I thought): read the Southwest airline magazine from cover to cover or listen to the Audible book I had downloaded to my phone. I picked up my phone and it wouldn't play my book. Guess who forgot to hit the download button after purchasing said book earlier that morning.

The plane finally started taxiing down the runway after the captain explained that due to the overweight fuel capacity, we would have to stay below a certain altitude, which would increase the turbulence a bit. Here's where this story becomes interactive. Please go ahead and insert every single cuss word you can think of and have them all spinning wildly around in mad circles above your head and then you might come close to what I felt like in that moment. Also insert mantra through gritted teeth, "Release, release, release, releeeeeeeaaaassssseeee." I found it all very ironic, though. This was seriously one of those, "God, it's me, Tina" moments. My attention was gotten, and so left to my own devices, (pun intended), I broke out the pen and paper.

I stared at it as we started to gain speed. I chomped away at my gum and had my water bottle on standby to combat the massive amount of ear-popping I saw in my future. My heart and the plane both lifted at the same time. *Release, release, release.* I began to replay the last breakout session at the conference over in my head to distract myself from the plane and the paper blankly staring back at me.

It was hard to believe in that moment that I was the same girl who used to write so feverishly every chance she got. It was hard to remember the student that edited her school's literary magazine, wrote for the newspaper, edited copy on the side, and had kept journals for decades. I still to this day have the endless journal entries replaying all the wonderful moments of meeting Heath in high school, our first kiss, his singing "Walking in Memphis" to me on the dock behind our high school, and the teenage angst of heartbreak when he gently let me know he didn't "love me that way". *Where was that girl's voice?* I asked myself. She was present during the event's breakout session when we had to become one with our paper and pen. She was on it one hundred percent when we had to deep-dive and expound upon the caged life, comfortable life, and the charged life.[2] I muttered under my breath, "I should start writing again."

The plane jolted hard left and my phone fell off my lap as I lay my other hand atop my journal. My reverie was broken, but my mind was intrigued by the question I arrived at. Where did my voice go over all these years? Where was the woman who passionately loved to write, read, listen to music, hike, have four-hour conversations about the future and her academic goals? When did I become so silent, and why had I? That would be a question worth pondering and answering. Bozinga! I could brain dump on that!

---

2   *Brendon.com,* "Caged, Comfortable, and Charged Life – Which Life is Yours?," YouTube Video, 9:39, February 13, 2014, https://www.youtube.com/watch?v=Mae9Vg9O6N4&feature=emb_title.

CHAPTER 2

THE PENDULUM

In the silence, there is a false sense of calm and control. I had needed that calm and that control when I was a little girl of five running with my baby brother up the stairs to hide from the screaming and things being thrown again. My voice only made things worse when it asked questions my mommy couldn't answer. I needed the stoic silence when my now ex-husband apologized for bruises around my neck, again. I needed the control that silent tears gave me when I raged inside that no one picked up the phone to tell me my uncle had died of pancreatic cancer until he was dead and buried. My quieted voice served its purpose the day my college advisor informed me that I could disenroll from the college and leave quietly or be expelled for my inebriated actions on the out-of-state field trip. Having no voice kept me safe. It let others dictate who I was, how I was, when I was, and it then also made it all their fault, not my own.

Within my silence was the most insidious lie of my entire being. It purposefully hid beneath the surface of me and reinforced the belief that I would have no say in anything. My well-maintained lie stated, "You will always and forever be a victim in your own story." That lie required back up and proof just the same as any lie does in order to stay in place.

We all have lies. Little ones, big ones, in-the-background ones, elephant-in-the-room-sized ones. They are within us until we choose to see them and learn to release them. They serve their purpose until we unpack and experience them, acknowledging that they no longer serve our greatest good. Once we walk all of those transitional steps, we step into radical gratitude for the experience and opportunity to evolve.

My lie kept me seeking silence as a defense mechanism to all my traumas. Your lies may have you doing one of these three actions: being stoic and silent, rebelling as a front cover, or running from yourself, in no specific order. I did all three over time. Given the circumstances at hand, you may come in and out of any one or combination of them as they continue to serve their purpose in your life of survival.

I was born into many lies that were not yet my own. From the start, my mother was marrying her sister's fiancé and they were having little ole me. How's that for a birth announcement? From this set of circumstances that were entirely out of my control, I came to believe and then seek out the proof that I was unintended, unwanted, and therefore of little value. This was a learned lie that I adopted as I grew up. It was a part of my foundation from the very beginning, and I sought out all the ways fathomable to uphold it. I grew into a willing participant that kept these lies watered and deeply rooted, and then passed them on. It took me several life-changing moments to realize the depths of pain that my lies were causing—not only to myself but to those I loved.

I don't want that for you or anyone else. You have carried lies for far too many years now, and I know how heavy and permanent they may feel. I want to assure you that it is time to leave them behind, that it is possible to have a vibrant, inspiring, and beautiful life! I've been unpacking my bags and moving into my life on purpose for almost nine years now, and that's what I have found to be true. It seems a silly thing to say, "Move into your life." It's what's needed, though. Our lives are filled with opportunities we miss along the way because of other people's traumas that we take on ourselves and never let go of. These set the soil for us to plant ourselves in the pain, dysfunction, and darkness of protecting the lies instead of living our truth in the sun. We lose sight of our own extraordinary. It took me a very long time, but I found mine again on a four-flight back home.

The flight ahead of me now that we were finally in the sky was life-changing. My voice rang so loud in my ears! Was it the roaring of the plane or the whiskey in my coffee making everything so loud inside my mind? As the pen hit the paper, my words came spilling out of a floodgate I didn't know I had been building for years. In that moment, I saw something else about my lies and how they had limited me. I had spent so many years of my life looking for roadblocks to protect myself from instead of clearing my own path. I acted out of fear with everyone I interacted with on a day-to-day basis. That was in direct, constant contrast to what I tried to present myself as in life. As I continued to write that day, I understood why I saw everyone else's life as so extraordinary, full of potential, and valuable. I believed that a life worth living was meant for everyone *except for me*. In the effort to maintain my lies about who I thought I really was, I had become so focused on finding the bumps and blockades in life's road that I had fucking become the greatest obstacle of all, keeping me from seeing my own potential, value, and true self! I had spent years so petrified of living that it became easier to keep everything inside, to just lie and not let anyone know how much I was struggling at home, at school, at work, in my marriage, or alone in the grocery store trying to buy milk. I just packed away all the pain, quite literally, and moved it from house to house.

Realizing that you have lied to yourself is heart-wrenching and freeing, all in one fell-swoop. It's like a pendulum that swings back and forth across your life. Everything behind you gets released as the pendulum swings back across the pain you've held all those years and you actively forgive yourself. Everything in the future becomes joyful and possible with new potential as the pendulum swings forward across years yet to come. And then, as it comes to rest in the center, your present, you feel the weight lift from your chest, you feel the anchors release from your feet. In that exact moment, a part of your heart opens, and you feel the sunshine on your face for the first time in so long you can't even remember. And in the embers of sunshine and joy, there are tingles of angst and knowledge that your lifetime has been shaped by misunderstandings and self-fulfilled prophecies as you have received and created the very life you focused on that entire time.

I focused on the avoidance of pain and disarray, and that's what I brought about. It's what I knew to look for because of my upbringing and all the learned behaviors. It was also what I was responsible for uncovering, unpacking, experiencing, releasing, and finding radical gratitude for afterwards.

The newly felt sunshine feels amazing and hopeful. It warms your nose and your forehead, and as you run your hand through your hair, you can feel the tingles of heat graze against your fingers. And life feels so incredibly possible. I could feel it that evening on the plane at 30,000 feet in the air. My spirits were literally high, and for the first time in my entire life, I understood why I had begun to lie to myself so much and how the lies stopped me from growing into this woman for as long as it did. Some might say I had an epiphany. Others might reference my plane ride as a cathartic moment. I was celebrating hardcore inside my soul and joyously embracing my arrival. That cathartic epiphany was inhaled deep, and right as the roar of accomplishment started to reach my brain, my heart acknowledged one very present tense lie that I was still telling.

CHAPTER 3

DÉJÀ VU

Instantly, I was catapulted back to when I was pregnant with my first child. The memories of a line dividing me inside came rushing back in with relief, recognition, and self-betrayal. All I had felt that night came back and washed over me as I sat in my window seat suspended in air and time transcribing my life on the pages in front of me.

This next part is what I would consider to be a trigger. If you are reading this or listening to it, take some time away from being around the kids or in the middle of an office space. This is what poured out of my soul that night as I returned my pen to the paper and continued to fly through the sky towards my homecoming...

I lied to you. My heart and spirit were broken. I was not fine. I would never be fine. I no longer understood how to live. I no longer recognized myself or how to find the remnants of who I thought I was before it all. I didn't matter; it wasn't about me anymore. Inside of me, I could feel you and I knew something grander and more than my own being was taking place. But I was lying to you while you grew inside of me, next to my heart. You heard the beat of my brokenness and you swam inside my soul for nine months, growing your heart, mind, lungs, fingers, and toes. With two words, I became your protector, and I only had nine months to figure out how to save us.

The only way I could keep us together made me lie to myself and everyone around us. You were doing amazing. You were growing strong legs that kicked me incessantly every night. You serenaded me with hiccups after every crazy meal I craved. Shrimp and mashed potatoes with gravy was our favorite—brown gravy was the best. Every time we went in to hear your heartbeat, I burst with joy. You were a gift and I couldn't wait to hold you. I couldn't wait to see what innocent perfection really looked like. I was going to tell you the truth once you were out. Once I knew you were OK and I could show you the new world I was planning for us, it would all be OK. I believed it would all come together. I would bring you into this world and the greatest miracle that you and I had pulled off together would make him stop hurting us. He loved you. He had to love me for carrying you. He also loved whiskey. And I naively assumed there was an easy choice to make.

I knew from the start I should not be with this man and that the insane amount of traumas connecting us should have sent me running in the opposite direction. The drugs and alcohol that daily inundated us kept me in a confused and panic-driven state of mind that those two words, "You're pregnant" shook me right out of immediately. It was huge thumb thwap to the forehead with the memo reading loud and clear: "It's time to grow up". I had to make a choice.

I was seven months along with you when I saw it was time to stop lying to you and to myself. It was a very bad morning. He locked us in the house and closed all the blinds at 7 a.m. He was irrationally drunk and didn't know who I was. I didn't know this version of him. You couldn't see his hands close around my neck, but I know you heard me beg for your life, not mine. That began my descent into the greatest lie of all. I no longer was going to fight for myself. I was not worth as much as you were. He could no longer hurt me if I wasn't acknowledging the pain or the fear of the pain. If I was solely protecting you, he wouldn't hurt me. I disconnected. I cast my lie over my life to protect us both.

Blood ran down my legs as I ran from him. I had kicked him in the balls, and he grabbed my neck. As I turned to grab my cell phone and run for the bathroom, he kicked his leg out and I fell stumbling against the table, and then the wall. It was an ugly blue wall, now splattered with red. He had our brown-handled onion-chopping knife in his hand and told me to sit down. He took my phone and I pleaded for him to calm down, to talk to me, to remember who I was and then I pointed to you inside my giant beach ball of a belly.

He was angry I had come home so late and accused me of being with another man. I had just finished my twelve-hour overnight shift at the residential treatment home I was a house manager for and came home to change my clothes, shower, and try to take a nap before going back to work. He had been out all night getting high on meth, and the beer and whiskey on his breath was the attempt to bring his high under control. I could feel something wet on my legs. It was the warmth of blood oozing down and

I didn't know if I was bleeding or if you were. He wouldn't let me move away from the wall I was slumped against. He kept pacing back-and-forth. Like a wild animal, he just kept looking at the blinds and back at me. Waving the knife in my face, he demanded to know whose dick I was out sucking. Over and over again he called me a whore. That was the first time I'd ever been called such foul names. I didn't know what the word "cunt" even meant. I didn't understand what was happening or why, but I knew I needed to save you. I needed to find out where the blood was coming from. I knew pregnant people don't bleed unless it was bad.

I had put my hands and shoulder out in front to keep you from hitting the wall, so my belly was safe, but I know you felt the jarring. I know you could tell the difference between me rubbing my belly talking to you about our dream life and this chaotic disarray. I was sorry and scared for you, so I began a new lie. I told him I needed to pee. I told him I was a whore, that I was sorry, that I understood why he was mad, and that I deserved to be punished. I asked if I could please pee and then I could pack my stuff and leave him alone. My lie didn't work. He got madder and yelled how right he was and waved around the knife in my face as he closed his eyes and began screaming at me. He screamed about how twisted women are and how I was no different.

It was OK. I saw my moment and while his eyes were closed, I lunged all of me towards him and knocked him over. He fell at least 4 feet away and I think you helped me push him away with my big old belly protruding out. I saw my phone on the counter and I ran for it while he laid still on the ground. The knife had gone flying out of his hand when he smashed down on the floor. I kicked it farther away and then ran to the bathroom. I locked the door and climbed into the bathtub. I was shaking. My shorts were soaked. I think I pissed myself. I leaned up against the shower wall and began talking to you, but it may have also been to myself as well. "It's OK," I said. "You're OK." I was not OK, but you had to be.

Slam. He threw himself against the door. The door itself ached and looked like it was going to fly off its hinges. I called 911 from the bathtub. I waited as he slammed himself over and over again against the door, screaming his new name for me. "You fucking whore, you dirty cunt, you filthy fucking woman." It took thirty-seven kicks before I heard the banging at the front door. I counted the number of times you kicked me as I waited for help. I knew you were OK because you were moving at hyper-speed in there. The blood was from my leg. He had somehow sliced my inner thigh when he attacked me. When he wrestled me to the ground, my head was facing away from him. All I saw was the floor coming so I had to brace my fall before my belly hit the floor. You were going to be OK no matter what he did to me.

That was the lie I would tell over and over again with each one of you. When the police came, I could hear the scuffling. I could hear them pinning him to the ground and his screams begging them to stop hurting him. I heard him yell, "Leave that bitch bleeding."

The officer who knocked on the bathroom door said, "It's OK. You can open the door now. We have him in custody."

23

As I opened the door and walked out into my living room, holding my belly, I apologized. "I'm so sorry I had to call you, he's not usually this bad." An officer said she was going to take my pictures, I protested. They took him away screaming, and now they wanted to take pictures to prove how bad my bruises were?! I didn't want to have proof because they might use it to take you away from me. I was fine. I was OK. And so are you. I just needed help this time. It got out of hand and wasn't going to again. This had never happened before to this extent. I just needed to talk to him when he was sober.

They had the ambulance medics restrain him and take him away because of how high he was. An officer gave me a pamphlet and tried to explain I could press charges. "I fell," I said. The officer knew I was lying. In the moment, I had no idea the truth would set me, you, and so many more after you, free. She tried to tell me my options. She continued to take pictures of my face, my neck, my arms, my legs, my back, and my hands. But not my belly. You were safe.

They wanted to transport me to the hospital, but I refused. My face was swollen. My lip was busted. My right eye was bloodshot and had a cut at the eyebrow. As I looked in the mirror, I remembered my car accident from the year before. My face wasn't that bad. I could remember a time far worse, another time I had felt equally as trapped. Staring in the mirror at that moment it felt like a Universal Déjà vu. I remembered how the nurses wouldn't let me see my face because they said I needed to heal up a little bit first. I had lied that day, too. I was supposed to go to school, but I chose to go to a party instead. That's not something I would've ever done before, but I was so damn tired of doing everything I was "supposed to" do in my life. For once I just wanted to have fun and be free from all the lying.

CHAPTER 4

LAST DAY OF TRUTH

As I sat in the passenger seat of my boyfriend Jimmy's Mustang, I shook with excitement and nerves. I'd never done anything like this before. I was so ready to embrace newfound courage and complete abandon. It was raining heavily that day, but we didn't care. There were five of us in the car, all going to the party, all ready to have fun and enjoy the day. We drove so fast down Woodsboro Road. We had already stopped for beer, and we just needed to grab a wallet before we headed out. "Faster, catch up to them," was the last thing I remember hearing before my entire life turned upside down. I was seventeen years old.

I felt like I was waking up from a nap. My head and eyes hurt, though. It seared like no headache I had ever experienced before. I reached up to wipe my brow, but my arm wouldn't move. Warm liquid oozed across my face and dripped into my eyes. My eyes felt heavy. A man's face blurred in front of me. He looked kind. He slowly came into clearer view, and I could see his mouth moving. I clearly heard each word of the calm and comfort that he spoke out loud to my mind.

I was not comprehending that I had been in a car accident. I was not privy to the knowledge that my placement in the car made it quite impossible for another physical soul to be in front of me at that moment saying, "You're OK," and then smiling back at my very confused self. That recalled moment was my mortality motivation and the reminder, from what I call "my High Advisor," that there was more to this life than I was allowing.

The voice repeated, slowly, enunciating each word, "You're OK, breathe for me." I blinked and tried to move, but still couldn't. My incomprehension continued. I started to hear screams. Again, I saw this man's kind face and his lips moving as he kept saying, "Breathe, it's OK, you're OK." Another voice rang out and I recognized that one…

"Tina, are you OK? Wiggle your hands, say something if you're OK." I thought, *Why's Jimmy asking if I'm OK? Of course, I was OK. We were headed to the party. Why am I so cold, and why is there water dripping all over me?* I was freezing and wet and sleepy and heavy. I had just woken up from a nap but was so sleepy still.

Then it hit me: this wasn't a nap. *What in the world is happening to me? Why are there so many people screaming? It is so loud! Why does my face hurt and where are my teeth?* I felt cold and scared, and it was dark. *Is this shock?* I asked myself. *Did I fall? Am I dreaming? Am I drowning? Did something happen?* Out of nowhere I felt myself being lifted up, like straight up, all of me at the same time. And then I heard a man say, "Darlin', we are going to take a little ride now."

I asked back, "Who are you and where am I?" *Why do I remember a saw sound?* I thought. *What was wet and why do I smell smoke? What was on fire? Where are my friends?*

Why do I hear a helicopter? Is anyone going to answer any of these questions? I remember saying, "Sir, I don't fly, I'm actually very scared of heights."

"You're not today, darlin'," he said. "We gotta fix you up!"

"Fix me up?!" What's wrong with me? I thought to myself. *Why was my boyfriend just standing there and how did his glasses get broken? What the fuck is going on and where am I?* I believe I had passed out at the point I was put on the helicopter. On Rt. 550, where the railroad tracks were, there was a point to curve sharp right, but the visibility and speed had been so poorly accounted for that Jimmy, as Susan C. Nicol would write in the *Frederick News Post* "failed to negotiate a curve," and we went soaring. In the picture shared on the February 24, 1995 article, you can see the upside-down remains of an adventure gone epically wrong. It was also the beginning chapter of the rest of my life.

In a split second, we swerved off the road and flew through the air, Jimmy's Mustang went flying, clipping the top five feet of a telephone pole, and then cleared an embankment, only to hit and roll several times down a hill to then crash upside down in the backyard of someone's home, where an oak tree finally stopped the car from sliding further into their back door. I had smacked my head on the window and slammed my jaw against the door. I free-fell in the car as it hit and rolled over and over. I thankfully did not have my seatbelt on as it smashed the roof level with the car's glove box. I had somehow flipped upside down with my face under the dashboard and my legs stretched into the backseat as my spine twisted. I fractured the T-12 vertebra, broke my jaw, and sliced open my forehead.

I remember begging the nurses not to take those scissors to my brand-new jeans. Just like I begged them for a mirror so I could see why everyone that came to visit me at Baltimore Shock Trauma kept having the same aghast look on their faces. Purple, blue, and red were meant to pigment sunrises, not skin. What I could see of my face was so swollen you couldn't tell it was a human face. The amount of swelling to both of my eyes made me look like I had been sucker-punched with one of those whack-a-mole paddles from the arcades.

The nurses lied to me and told me that everything was just fine. Who the fuck tells you everything is just fine while people are looking at you like you've been beaten within an inch of your life?

That was a question I asked myself at seventeen. It turned out to be the same question I would ask myself for nine years as I allowed a man to consistently beat the shit out of me and console myself with the lie. "Everything is just fine." Freedom doesn't come from lies. It took me over twenty years to find that out completely.

I spent my entire senior year of high school trapped in a back brace that sat just above my pelvic bone and went up around my shoulders. While I had survived, I was trapped inside my mind and my body. I had to go back home to the woman I had run from. I had to do the exact same thing again as I looked in my bathroom mirror a year and a half after the accident, now pregnant and protecting you.

You were going to come out and meet the world in less than three months and I needed help. I couldn't just keep lying to you or myself, or to anyone else for that matter. My mom was the last person I wanted to ask for help, but she was the only person I could call. She bought me a one-way plane ticket from Albuquerque back to Maryland and sent my stepfather to pick me up from the airport. I packed everything I could and promised you we would be OK, that we would figure it all out.

It was not OK. She looked me in the face and gave me an ultimatum I couldn't even comprehend. "Give him up for adoption and you can stay here at home." I had only seen your face at the doctor's appointments. I only knew you through your heartbeat. But I knew you were mine! I hadn't yet held you or smelled you or seen your beautiful blue eyes, but I knew you. I knew how you would feel. I knew who you would grow to be. I knew the boy I would get to raise and the man that would one day bless this world because God gave him to me to look after. I knew who I would be in that exact moment. And I knew my blessing would be in raising you, loving you, and one day leading you to soar free on your own. I did not ponder. I did not stall. I did not think on it. I said, "No. He is mine, and I am no longer yours." I was nineteen and petrified, but I was completely positive that you were the only choice to choose.

CHAPTER 5

COMFORT IN THE CHAOS

That was the last day I told the truth, to anyone. I had no idea what I was going to do, but I knew I would figure it out. My grandmother opened her home to me and took me shopping for maternity clothes. The month I stayed with her was filled with phone calls, arguments, and pleadings from Jesse that I would come back to Albuquerque and the hope that doing so would be a best next step.

The promises came and went rapidly. I continued to hold onto the lies out of comfort and eventually complacency. With each passing day, month, year, and child I would try to come at the disease of alcoholism, the current day's physical anguish, and the plethora of childhood traumas from a new understanding. My resiliency kept my chin afloat with the perpetual hope that "maybe; one day…" My faith, though wavering, kept me grounded and reminded me that I could not repeat the mistakes of my mother. I wanted a two-parent household. I wanted a partner to raise children with together. I wanted unconditional love given and received.

Unconditional love means affection without limitation, love without condition. It does not mean unconditional acceptance of inflicted pain, neglect, and disrespect physically and emotionally. I blurred those meanings. I lied to myself, claiming that *my* unconditional love for Jesse meant I needed to accept him, all of him, his faults, and his fists.

While I was in Maryland, Jesse made all the promises my heart needed to hear in order for me to justify within myself that it would be better to return than it would be to stay, alone and raising a newborn. Months after we had our first child, we thought that moving away from Albuquerque to Alamogordo, New Mexico, would help our relationship. We would be away from the addiction triggers, away from the rest of his tumultuous family, and closer to his biological sister. Months after that, we found out that I was pregnant again. He had been stringing together more weeks of sobriety, had started a fantastic full-time job, and we were incrementally mending our barbed-wired fences.

There were days of joy. There were memories I can still smile back on today, like my oldest winning a baby-derby with a Spider-Man walk, my second son crawling inside the guitar case and sitting upright to watch his dad play Stevie Ray Vaughn riffs. The day he held our oldest daughter in his arms for the first time and locked eyes with me was beautiful. When our next son had to be rushed back into the hospital at just seven days old and we prayed together that he would be healed and come home, there was joy. When we had our fifth child, and I knew with certainty that naming her after the Serenity Prayer was meant to be, there was joy.

Interlaced in there were the darker memories, the real-life replays of my own Dr. Jekyll and Mr. Hyde. The consistent inconsistency and lack of emotional stability became the foundation I raised my children on and the *normal* I leaned on daily. I got really good at reading his moods, the energy in the air, and even better at hiding my emotions. A subconscious behavior habit that carried me through my childhood was also feeding my adult lie that, *"It's OK, it's all OK."* Those moments when I was the five-year-old racing up the stairs with my brother in tow gave me behavior breadcrumbs to follow and survive with well into my adult years. Those behavior breadcrumbs didn't nourish my children any more than they did me. They only acted as a filler.

We moved back to Albuquerque to be closer to his family and let them try to help as we started our life together over again with new expectations from one another and new responsibilities as soon to be parents of three. I still held out hope that I could "fix" things, that it would get better, and we'd be a real family. While he started attending intermittent counseling sessions, the occasional AA meeting and I was working fulltime again, the gnawing at my being was always the truth that I needed to leave. I needed to escape. And those truths were always mowed down by the traumatic momentum that comes with violence, rape, lies, drugs, alcohol, and the denial of all of it in the dire pursuit for "real love and acceptance."

On the surface, everything looked as picturesque as I painted it. It also felt deceivingly hopeful. But I was only going through the motions of my disconnected daily surviving. Every moment spent with my boys grew me and made me long for a better situation for all of us.

When I couldn't find enough comfort in my home life, I began searching for outlets. Just like when I was younger, I poured myself into school because it was a qualifiable safety that no one but me could take away. This time, I thought, it could be the answer out of this trap. It was my distraction from the pain, a beneficial choice for my someday career, and the only exit strategy I could attempt without him figuring it out.

I wanted out. I was dying and my children were watching him kill me. At four years old, my oldest son would peak around the corners at the dismantling of his little life and his three-year-old younger brother would come running full-speed trying to linebacker-style drop his father at the knees to get him away from me. I knew then I had to remove us from the damage that was continuing. I understood he was not changing, and I knew I couldn't continue to see the looks of confusion in my babies' eyes as they tried to make peace inside their little heads of the daily disasters unfolding. I arrived at the concrete decision to leave numerous times. Each time was met with equally, at the time, compelling disasters that would ensue if I tried.

After having my third child, I had started the process to join the Peace Corps. I was excited that there was real hope for me and my three little ones. I opened up a separate checking account. I began to let a friend close enough to me that I didn't feel utterly alone. I still felt trapped, but the windows were opening. I overlooked all of the daily fights, frustrations, paycheck-chasing, relapses, electricity shut-offs, hidden bottles of whiskey in the insulation of the garage walls, and I even kept quiet about his stash of bottles inside the dryer drum for the machines he was "working on" to sell. I dealt with each drunken rage at the time it happened, pushed the kids in their rooms, and kept myself and the kids away from home as much as possible. I always tried to keep focusing on just making it through another day. My past was dismissed and my future forgotten. But I had finally set a plan in motion.

The Peace Corps would give me the education and connections to resources my kids and I all needed. I had gotten Jesse to agree to it as a part of my furthering my education so I could continue supporting us with a better job while he could take the time to go to (yet another) rehab. I didn't care what he believed as long as he wasn't aware of what I was hoping to do after completing my degree. But my focus was severed, and my exit strategy ended with another positive pregnancy test that then disqualified me from joining the Peace Corps because I would "age out" of eligibility by the time I gave birth.

I temporarily postponed finishing my degree again. Instead, I started working at a drug and alcohol rehab as a part of the "Working to Well-being" assistance program. It was only a temporary position, but there I got to see inside the after-care for this disease slowly killing me and my five children. I had front row seats to the detox that wasn't happening at home. And I landed again in "I know the kids and I cannot stay in this anymore, period, end of story." I went down the list of all the reasons I couldn't make it on my own and paired those up with all of his reminders that he would find us and take them and they'd never see me again. It was always the way he phrased that last statement that scared me most. Why would they never see *me* again? Why wasn't he phrasing it the other way?

I wasn't as much crushed as I was confused. That began a time of spiritual exhaustion inside me. How could any God want to keep me in this maelstrom? What was I doing to continuously deserve this lot in life, and what could possibly account for now four lives being brought into this dysfunction? And it would happen one more time. I had another baby a year after my fourth child. Life began to substantially change for my kids and me during that fourth pregnancy and very soon after. During my pregnancy with my fourth child I had started attending Al-Anon meetings and couples therapy sessions, and I enrolled part-time again at the community college. My head was just far enough above water that I began to find hints of myself. I gained the confidence to start asking for more than the pain. I found hope again when I talked Ilene, the owner of Sandia Learning Center, into hiring me as kitchen help two months before I was due for the fourth time.

I had noticed that Ilene was always the one making meals. In a passing conversation after one of my 3 pm to 11 pm shifts, we chatted as she helped me out to the car with a sleeping baby girl on my one shoulder and my two boys following at her heels. In my heart, I was praying again. She answered that prayer the night I began my cooking adventures for her 120-kid day-care center. It was the perfect solution to our safety, sanity, and bank account.

I could be with the kids *and* make a paycheck. I thrived in the daycare environment, being surrounded by my babies, safely. I could "extend" my shift so I didn't have to take us home. I could sneak us all out of the house and come in early if Jesse had an especially horrible night before. I was often sent home with many of the meals that were left over "so it doesn't go to waste." And while I was enrolled in school, I could confidently attend my classes without the worry of the kids being with Jesse. I went back and forth with the guilt of having them all there sometimes from open to close. But they were safe. They were fed amazing meals that I cooked in between classes that first year, and they were adored and loved on by the teachers and the center owner that became family to me. God gave me much to be radically grateful for through this time of transition.

I was afforded the time and space to grow emotionally, physically, and professionally. The owner took us completely under her wing. She adored my babies and spoiled them every chance she could. Some days I would finish and grab up all the diaper bags and put my oldest daughter on my hip to gather the oldest two boys from the pre-school only to be told they were "getting snack with Ilene." I'd smile the whole way walking back to the office and then find them in their makeshift desk-fort splurging on graham crackers and milk with Ilene sitting next to them at the computer. My daughter would lunge into Ilene's arms, knowing she was getting a snack, snuggles, and a kiss before we left to go home for bed. I was grateful.

I had my fourth baby February 13th, the day after Ilene's birthday. She knew I was coming back to work as soon as I possibly could, physically. She turned the food pantry into a nursing room for me and Halo, the office assistant who became one of my best friends. Halo was pregnant at the same exact time, and our due dates were days apart. It's been nineteen years, but we still joke to this day about the poor teachers that survived our hormones, one of whom was also pregnant. Kami delivered a month later and is still a confidant and best friend to me today. She became the little sister I didn't have, given all my other circumstances, and a cornerstone reminder that I was loved.

When I came back seven days after having my son, Ilene let me know that she hired a cook and offered me the Day-care Program Director position. The agreement was that she would cover my certification class in exchange for my continued employment at the center and assistance in opening a second site. I eagerly agreed. As I learned what it meant to be an office assistant, I also helped in the summer program with the school kids, which gave me the opportunity to actually play with my oldest two boys. As my kids continued to happily be at Sandia from open to close each day, I was getting to experience and enjoy all of my babies so much more.

We were all safe inside those daycare walls. I laughed with this family. And my tears were from the overwhelming joy that I felt as Ilene blessed us with clothes, food, and school supplies as the kids kept needing more than my paycheck could keep up with. Working at that center was a gift. On my breaks I would hold my newborn, watch my oldest boys run and ride tricycles on the front playground, and then walk down the hall to the back of the building to see my daughter squealing down the slide. I went on every field trip I could. We went to the zoo, water park, and planetarium that summer. Our days started with breakfast around a classroom table, dodging fallen bowls of eggs, cereal, and fruits, and ended with the family-style meal with about forty kids, all hungry, hyper, and waiting to go home.

Not my four though. They knew we stayed after dinner and "helped." Our routine was easy, simple, and safe. My newest addition most days slept in between feedings in the baby room or in my arms as I walked the center, and sometimes in the car seat by my feet in the office. My three oldest always waited patiently for their snack savior to come retrieve them from their classes. And I would work on my papers for school in between closing classrooms down and signing teachers out for the day. There was no Jesse in this part of our story. And that was why it had begun to feel so good. I was experiencing more joy than pain on a daily basis.

Five months into my newfound semblance of stability, the thoughts of leaving trickled in again. I had finally qualified for Section 8 Housing and could "afford" my rent without any worries about the paychecks Jesse continued to drink, snort, or straight up lose. My day care vouchers, food stamps, financial assistance, and bank accounts were all under just my name. Since Jesse continued to take off on drunken benders weeks at a time, I was allowed to remove him "from the household". He was gone in name but not in impact.

He got sober, got a new job, started counseling again, and went on medication. We moved houses, and I started feeling like he was just the devil I knew. Through another round of IOP (intensive out-patient), he maintained a month and a half of sobriety. He worked on himself and I did the same. I began to like myself again. I arrived at a space inside myself emotionally where I saw the patterned behaviors happening again. All the changes were not going to remove the violence from our lives. All the Band-Aids sticking to us were not going to stop the bleeding out of our souls. Not for us or for him. He needed help I couldn't give. I wanted a safe place to grow and thrive with my children that he always dismantled. I had made up my mind but there would be yet another plot twist.

My youngest was barely seven months old when I went back for the scheduled leap procedure on my cervix to remove the cancer they had found. The pre-op blood work relayed that I was unable to go through with that procedure, though. I was standing in the circle in front of Presbyterian Hospital listening to my OB tell me over the phone, "Tina, you're pregnant."

We had sex one time in that seven months. Once. I said yes one damn time. I was dumbfounded, delirious, and in denial. We drove home in silence. He didn't know all my plans went out of the proverbial tub with the baby and the bathwater. I felt myself shrinking inside and starting to disconnect again from myself and my reality. The kids were at the day care already, so I let them stay to give myself the time to rapidly process, throw myself on my floor and sob, and frantically begin to ask *why* to whatever God was listening. At this point I would have welcomed Buddha, Jesus, and the Tree of Life if any one of them would just answer my prayers.

Sitting alone on the steps outside my house, I thanked God for such a beautiful gift and another opportunity to love unconditionally. Nine months later, after I knew that I knew I was closing this chapter of my life and that I just needed to take the steps away from it, I chose the Serenity Prayer to guide me. I fell deeply in love with yet another child and with being a mother. I drummed up all the hopes my perpetual optimism could muster, and I demanded all the "fixes" be front and center. I asked, "God, grant me the serenity to accept the things I cannot change, the courage to change the things I can, and the wisdom to know the difference."

I stayed. I stayed nine years too long is what my battered mind and body acknowledged. But I walked away at long last with five of God's greatest reminders that there was more life to be lived and we only had to choose to do so. Through all my years, I had learned how to stay in the pain and become best friends with it, anticipating its arrival and actually mourning its departure. My learned behavior to deny pain kept me in a cycle of it. It taught my children not to trust their own intuition. And it kept us at arm's-length as they innocently understood the juxtaposed moments that framed their lives. They understood that I was lying every time they asked me, "Mommy, are you OK?" And I responded with "Mommy's fine" every time.

Trauma has a way of migrating to the underbelly of us all. In my writing and releasing of this pain, I was able to see the patterns that stemmed from my childhood feelings of being out of control of my environment and the people in it. I did not feel safe, secure, or valued. These feelings became core beliefs at such a young age that I operated from them autonomically. My rebellious acting out in college, financial splurging of the medical settlement from my car accident, and majoring more in the bar down the street rather than the studies I had received a full ride for was a short-lived attempt at me *surviving* life on my terms. Alas, I still wasn't *living* my life at all.

My overeating was one of the many ways I coped with not living. It was an attempt to gain control. Every food I chose was a choice and it filled me up with a false confidence and surety while weighing me down physically and emotionally. The false beliefs that silence, pretenses, and lies put me in control paralyzed my emotional growth and built a wall between me and those I loved most, specifically my children and the man I call best friend, husband, and soul mate today. Uncovering that and beginning to unpack the bag of lies released me from another self-imposed prison and the walls of false safety that I created in maintaining them. The third step of this process, "experience", gave way to conversations with Heath and each of my children that I never could have imagined would take place. Step four's direction of release was tangled in a web of lies that landed me owning the embarrassment and shame that I clung to out of comfort. The realization that staying in that comfort had become more painful than the discomfort of changing allowed me to see that the very things keeping me from feeling whole again and living my life were the things I was lying to myself about. You are probably wondering how in the world step five, radical gratitude, is going to be the end result, ever. I know I did.

You don't have to believe the lies. You don't have to hold on to the threads of sanity and try and weave together the tapestry that your heart aches for each night as you lay down your head. You can be tired, afraid, lost, distant, unaware, overwhelmed, and done. You can also be ready, brave, uncertain, willing, and present. Healing from trauma comes after you agree to the stand in the sun with the truths again.

If you, reader, are in any relationship and experiencing abuse, no matter how young or old you are, please seek help and support for yourself. Stop telling yourself that everything is fine when you know it is not. In the United States, you can call the National Domestic Violence Hotline at 1-800-799-7233.

Lying about being OK, and refusing to seek help or support, and pursuing a life I believed I was "supposed to" regardless of the pain filling up my bags, kept me from having deep personal relationships and experiences. Uncovering these lies was a turning point for me. Taking the time to unpack took the decision and commitment to live in the present not the pain. Choosing to willingly experience all the depths of emotions and truths buried beneath the lies requires dedication and integrity. Releasing the lies takes you down a broken road, but will bring you home where there is immense and radical gratitude for the life about to be fully owned and lived.

CHAPTER 6

THE WORK

I did finally make it home from that Phoenix trip. It took me the entire flight back to divinely download all those thoughts, memories, and realizations onto the paper. It felt like I was purging my soul that night. I knew it was something I needed to get out for me, but in writing it, I also saw how important it was going to be moving forward to the people closest to me. I knew this was something that I needed to share with my husband, as I had never completely opened up about it from this perspective. I needed to own what I had released so the people I was keeping trapped in it with me could also breathe freely once again.

So, I did mention earlier that I am a mom of seven? I've shared how I became a mom the first five times. I'd like to share the birth of my second "first" child, and my last baby as well. When Heath and I came together again ten years later and began a new life for me and my first five, it was a whirlwind of trying to keep them safe and me sane through all of the transitions. But we were elated to try for a baby. Heath had two pups and no children. He took on the world when he entered my life again and being able to give him the gift of a child of his own made my heart soar. And it made my blood pressure go through the roof with pre-eclampsia.

It also brought to light some of the other health issues I had put on the mental back burner, like the prescribed phentermine I had been taking to assist with my binge eating, which was having an adverse reaction in my body. The IUD that had been removed months earlier made it more difficult to conceive, whereas before I was jokingly referred to as "Fertile Myrtle." It took us months of trying but we made a "tadpole" and were overjoyed at the merging and growing of our new family together.

I was about three months along when I had my first scare. During all my other pregnancies, I was used to being fairly on my own. Heath was so supportive, loving, and proactive that I was thrown for an emotional loop. I didn't know how to embrace or connect with such love and care, and it brought up resistance in me. That came across to him as me being cold, angry, and more than just the hormonal chaos that pregnancy comes with. I struggled to let him care for me and brought much more stress and strain on my own plate than was ever necessary.

My lack of processing and debriefing from the previous trauma in my first marriage left me in a reactive loop. I kept pressing for my own sense of self and control so much so it was actually pushing him away. I was afraid to be vulnerable. I was afraid to *need* anyone; it hurt to trust. It caused emotional angst to believe that someone actually had me and was unconditionally supportive. It broke a part of my being that even as much as I loved Heath, I was petrified to be loved by him.

At three months along, I was in my office at work talking with my co-worker and stood up to run something out to a classroom and noticed that I had gushed something. I looked down and blood was trailing down my legs. I was rushed to the emergency room where Heath met me and there we waited to find out if there was still a baby inside of me to carry.

After definitely ruling out a miscarriage and placenta previa, the doctors found the bleed around my uterus. This led to my being remanded to bedrest. I had a chorionic bleed completely around my entire uterine wall so every time I sneezed, breathed heavy, or thought of moving, I gushed blood. The doctor's explicit instruction was rest, go to the bathroom and back, no standing for long periods of time, no sex, no exerting myself in any way, shape, or form. "And take your blood pressure daily for the next six months," he ordered.

Our very healthy baby boy was born after I was induced, and I got to experience true joy. The look in Heath's eyes as he held our child, his son, for the very first time was exhilarating. He beamed with pride and had such wide-eyed astonishment as he looked over the brand-new life staring back up at him. It was one of the most serene moments I'd ever experienced after the birth of one of my children. Heath had held my hand, snuck me Snickers, and wiped my tears, and I'm quite certain he would have been willing to have the contractions for me, too. That was the complete opposite of what all my previous pregnancies had been like. He stayed in the room the whole time. He actually missed the part where I pulled out our son and the nurse helped get him to my chest because he ran to the door to yell for a doctor when I could not hold back the push that was supposed to just be a cervical dilation check. He did not once leave my side for a smoke or to down a fifth of whiskey. His kisses of comfort were laced with love and admiration, not Southern Comfort or Marlboro lights.

The polarities of my world slowly came to a stop as each year kept on and I began to see more of my own dysfunctional behaviors playing out in my older children while witnessing the exact opposite in my "second-first" child. I was able to be more present with my newborn and could feel unfamiliar connections and maternal instincts that had been missing in me the first five times. As he grew into a toddler, there were moments of seeing my new life through his inquisitive eyes. There were emotional confusions inside me I didn't know how to share or put words to either.

The trauma-mind lies to you. From every angle needed, your mind's nook and crannies are repeatedly spackled with the tight caulking of finely beaded lies so you can't see outside the pain unless you physically choose to remove the emotional mask glued to your face. Identifying with the pain only circles you back into the lies that got you there. You can choose a new view. You can choose to remove the mask and the limited view it offered. You can step into your most powerful self and rise above it all.

It took me many, many years, tears, and miles, before I was willing to remove my mask. I wore my mask everywhere I went. It was as much a part of my identity as being a mother, a wife, a student, and friend. I hid safely on the other side of it, accepting the daily created numbness inside me. Like Groundhog Day, every day began and ended with the certainty of aloofness, disconnection, lack of empathy, layers deep of emptiness, and the tidal waves of anxiety, fear, and disappointment that the day again would be one not lived and only barely survived.

There was a gossamer-thin wall, a literal outer layer that stood between me and the life I was not experiencing. I could push my hands into it and press my mind's eye up against it. On rare occasions I could feel myself standing one foot in it and one foot out of it long enough to fully feel the smile from my heart up to my eyes when I held my children or watched them play. There were moments long enough to feel the kiss my husband set on my lips as he tried to pull me away from the cold, numb-normal I used to survive in amongst them all. I could observe my behaviors and understand the cold calculation of attempted control. And I could witness the replay of every yesterday-pain. But I could not breathe in enough air to fill my lungs with the current day's true tranquility.

I had to choose. I had to choose a path not walked every day back to the very pain and deception I trapped myself inside out of fear that I'd feel anything unidentifiable. What if I had felt joy? What if I had felt excitement? What would happen to me if I felt elation? I would have experienced an identity crisis. That's exactly what happened as the paradoxical pull of my youngest son teased my curiosity and opened a door. I saw opportunity and potential when watching my sixth child begin to question everything in his surroundings. I saw the child I once was long, long ago, reflected in his daily inquisitions of self and his place in his world.

"Why are you not up when the sun wakes up, Mommy?" Such an innocent, silly question to ask, but wise beyond his years. At barely two years old, the little boy with long, blond hair and eyes that reflected my own, raised questions that I stopped asking myself because the trauma and lies locked me in a holding pattern. Diving into the curiosity evoked happiness. Happiness led me towards joy. Joy opened up the possibility of feeling whole again. In my pursuit to release the ties and lies that kept me from experiencing my true, unmasked self, I was being more and more of the mom I had always wanted to be. It felt incredible and downright miraculous some days. I was seeing more than just glimpses of a happier, healthier me. I was connecting to a vibrant, grateful, optimistic being that wanted to lead and stay in place.

The inner critic inside of me was terrified and getting louder and louder, though. Every conceivable fuck-up was blasted inside my ears on a loop repeat, just like my mother had done with the news coverage of my car accident years ago. In the attempt to shame and blame me, I was picking up where she left off, replaying all the reasons why I was unworthy of anything resembling joy or unconditional love.

So I ran down the rabbit hole with self-inflicted inquisitions firing below-the-belt shots at my soul. My ego screamed, "What would happen if your son finds out that his Mommy was not the superwoman he grew up believing I was to him and all his older siblings? What if he found me out to be the once-abused, forgotten, lost, and angry woman who actually struggled to take him to the park and be around other people so he could play and feed the ducks?"

Those irrational fears were a part of the everyday anxiety I still experienced years after leaving the relationship and years into the healthy, safe, supportive, and loving one with Heath. I recreated pain for comfort. I stubbornly used my pain to keep everyone at an arm's-length from me. For a very long time, it was much more comfortable for me to stay in my pain than it was to come out and live with the people I was hurting.

To say that I am stubborn is an understatement, and I own that. The only person more stubborn than me is Heath. That sixth pregnancy had been a high risk one for me physically and a very emotional roller coaster for a first time Dad, but he was amazing. The care, support, effort, and resiliency he showed was extraordinary during all those months and the many years that followed them.

The years were filled with my fears, his fears, my physical limitations from a prolapsed uterus, gall-bladder surgery, an eventual hysterectomy, a severe complication after another surgery, and our emotional stalemating of one another as he grew tired of being pushed away and I fought to prove to myself he wouldn't stay, either.

He never stopped meeting me with compassion. He never left me or the kids. He never gave up on the friendship we started over twenty-five years prior. The compassion he met me with is one of the reasons I was able to uncover another one of my lies. Unpacking my belief that I was unworthy of unconditional love and that I would just wind up alone and abandoned again was a huge step away from the victim state of being. It is not just a state of mind. It encompasses you and dictates your very decisions on how to exist. I had refused to take that third step in the healing process and inadvertently recreated the fears that supported my lies, which then stagnated my healing process. I met his love with disbelief. His support could only be temporary and fair-weathered in my mind because of my choice of being.

I could have, just like you have the power to now, changed my mind. Remember, lies need lies to be maintained. Because I would not own the original emotions of the original traumas, I could not experience the emotions towards the needed release of those traumas. It took me years to release myself (and my family) from the ramifications and reactions that were built into that lie. But I arrived at that radical gratitude and as I began to intentionally feel it more days than I did not, it gave way to my being able to feel the unconditional positive regard. I began to believe in my own love story again.

CHAPTER 7

PATTERNS REPEATED

My sister was five years younger than me, and one of the goofiest kids ever. She freaking loved her cats and was obsessed with stealing my clothes when we were little. She had a beautiful mosaic calico kitty named Mojo that literally slept on her head. Twenty-five years later, I believe Mojo came back as the reincarnated cat that my oldest daughter picked at the pet shelter on the Friday I decided she needed a companion.

Shannon and I shared a room until her fifth birthday. When she was little, we shared matching pajamas, a love for ice cream, and as she got older, we shared secret ways of staying in touch when I moved out of the house and was forbidden to contact her or my brother. We were both adults and well into having children before we started connecting again, but we were both miles apart from being close siblings and even further apart from being friends.

The split that our mother created when we were both still kids left a large divide to be crossed before we knew who each other were in present times. But the fact that we were sisters gave us a door into trying to call on one another for what we both wished we could have had, had things been different.

Shani, as I called her, had struggled with drugs, alcohol, and depression for years. The abuse and neglect she had sustained took a toll on her greater than I ever truly knew about. Her youngest daughter was barely nine months old when she made the frantic call to me during my abnormal psychology class, begging me to come pick Livi up so no one would take her away. When I understood that she was not calling from her apartment thirty-five minutes away from me and actually was calling from Louisville, Kentucky, I knew things were bad.

My husband got up the next morning at 4 am and drove the eight hours to my sister, whom he had never met, and retrieved a niece I had only seen in the NICU and held for a moment. Alivia was so tiny. She had to be monitored as she detoxed from the drugs and alcohol my sister had used. It had been a tough pregnancy for her, and her habits of choice only complicated it further. We had conversations and visits as she got closer and closer to her due date, about how much she knew that she wanted more than what we had as children. That conversation came right back around again as my husband drove to rescue her little girl from her.

While he drove straight back, Shannon and I continued to talk on the phone and get the paperwork for me to pick up and have notarized from the local FedEx store. Unfortunately, given our known encounters with one another, I didn't trust her further than I could throw her, which left me feeling the dire need to officiate her request that Heath and I retain temporary custody of Livi for an extended period of time while she took care of her health and recovery.

During the mere week and a half that we had my beautiful niece, it fired inside Heath and me both a desire to have another baby of our own. It was a nasty custody battle that included another family that Shannon had also given custody permissions to for my niece. But justice for an innocent girl was served when Livi was adopted by two incredible loving parents who I still have the blessing to keep contact with today.

In that extremely brief moment in time we had opened our hearts and home to my niece, Heath and I decided to have one more child together. It didn't take nearly as long to get pregnant the second (seventh) time, but our entire world was about to shift again in ways neither of us could have imagined.

CHAPTER 8

SEVEN OF NINE

We got another purposeful eviction notice. My water was broken. The Pitocin coursed through my veins. I happily received an epidural. My rising blood pressure was closely monitored through the two days of contractions. Heath and I were ready to welcome another life into our world. That little life was ready to be here and teach lessons that often felt divinely aligned.

It took us until she was about six months old to find out she had been having longer and longer periods of fluid in her ears, leading to multiple ear infections. The reason she wasn't turning towards our voices when we talked to her was because she wasn't fully hearing us. Her lack of hearing led us to learning and growing so much. I had raised six children and never once did I struggle to actually speak to them. I had to learn a new way to mom. I was gifted the opportunity to learn a new way to hear all my children through this experience.

That little spitfire gave me a path towards more truth. Looking back, if you had told me that after having my seventh child I would not only be embracing the insanities that come with parenting, but that I would also be fighting high blood pressure again, post-partum depression for the third time, experiencing more PTSD from the years of abuse that I denied, and then also fighting to keep my marriage, I would have looked at you and said, "You are crazy," and reached for the remote and a bag of Doritos! Those were my realities, though. I needed to lie to myself and everyone else as well. All of that could not seriously be taking place. Not ten years into a fairytale reunion of finding my true love, my knight in shining armor who helped evacuate me and my first five kids out of a volatile marriage. Everything we endured could not possibly be headed into a divorce.

I'd like to say that I had no idea what was ahead of me or that I didn't know that all of everything I had survived was going to come to call. I'd like to believe I had no idea how my behavior made my husband feel distant and broken. I so wish I did not know my kids were losing out on amazing years with me, or I them, because it was so much easier for me to hide behind my packed bags of lies, the weight-gain, and the overwhelming sadness. I knew it was happening. I knew it was all spiraling out of my control right before my eyes. And that only made me lie to myself and others even more.

Let me introduce you to one of my little game changers, kiddo number seven: Isabella Rayne, aka Izzy, aka Bella, aka Midge (short for "Midget"). She was born with a mohawk full of dark locks and an umbilical cord longer than I am tall! She completed our family and became what I referenced and still giggle about today, as our "Seven of Nine." (*Star Trek: Voyagers* fans will appreciate this.) Bella was barely six weeks old and I had been feeling utterly disgusted with myself. I should just be bouncing back, right?

Yeah, no. I was feeding her in my recliner at 1 a.m., and as I looked down at the miniature miracle and leaned in to smell her little head, I was completely overwhelmed with both joy and pain. The joy of what her life could be and the pain of what it would be limited to if I stayed stuck in the emotional paralysis that had continued to grow in me.

Bella was my third girl, his first. We joked that we were totally hoping for another boy because of how much "easier" they are, but for me, it wasn't about them being easy or not. For me, it was honestly quite selfish. I wanted another boy because I was scared to have another girl. I never understood how to "click" with other girls. I didn't know how to relate to the emotions, thoughts, beliefs, or values that a girl gets raised with, as I didn't have that opportunity, and didn't want them to grow up and be anything like me. The history of violence in my family ran deep. Generations of women on both sides of my family tree were consumed by addiction, domestic violence, sexual abuse, co-dependency, depression, and an over-abundant aversion to habits of health and well-being. My mother was no more prepared than I was, raising babies as a baby. The emotional behaviors that were handed down through the females in my family terrified me. I understood the psychological ramifications of abuse and addiction, but sitting there holding another new life that I had been gifted the opportunity to bring into the world had me searching for a final end to the metastasizing disease of chaos and emotional rioting. These generational roots needed to be ripped up and out for good.

I held no understanding of my own value as a woman in this world. How was I supposed to teach my girls to be bold and brave if I was neither? I felt like a complete and utter hypocrite as a girl, as a woman, and as a person. My identity was a lie and the circumstances I surrounded myself with confirmed that identity. I wanted more, more for my children, more for me. An epic battle waged inside my mind as I understood that I wanted more than what my lies were allowing for all of us. On the surface, that sounds like an amazing and selfless act that any parent is "supposed to" pursue. There was another lie to uncover! There was a voice so quiet inside myself that I truly didn't recognize it as my own. Along this journey, I came to know her more. I learned how to listen to her and how to talk with her again, and I learned when she lied and why.

Inside of each of us resides the essence of who we always have been and were meant to be. That is not the same as the "supposed to" diatribe we trap ourselves into believing. For me, it started as this girl that never felt heard. She learned that silence kept her safe, but she wailed on the walls surrounding her, silently begging to be released, to be allowed to live amongst the living. Sitting there, holding my newborn in my arms, I had a moment of pure lucidity. That girl that I had grown so accustomed to hiding was momentarily reflected back to me in my daughter's eyes. She was breathtaking, and as much as I understood everything she would be capable of, I also sat with the fear that I would fail her and the little one in my arms. In that moment, I berated myself with inner dialogues that had plagued me since I was a child, asking relentlessly, *How am I going to fix the things I was failing my children in? How am I "supposed to" teach any of them to be a person I didn't know how to be?* It was in that seemingly nonchalant moment that the seeds of change were being planted inside my soul. New roots were branching out and the seeds I was finally capable of watering were about to sprout and grow. A healthier garden was possible. I was ready to unpack my bags and figure shit out.

The reflection of my potential self was enough to make me wonder why I could see that in her eyes and not my own, why yet again, as I looked into another of my children's beautiful new eyes, I could see more than just a maybe. It was the lie-lifting acknowledgment that what I wished for her in that moment and all the moments to come, was OK to wish for myself. The beliefs and values I wanted to instill in her and grappled to give my older children were also acceptable to want for myself! This was jarring to all my senses. It woke something up inside of me and began my quest for more life lived every day. I wanted to stand in my power, not just reach for that spot in my life anymore. It's what led me to start focusing on a growth mindset. I wanted more than what I was limiting myself to, and to give it to my children, I needed to first honor it in myself. The oxygen mask in the airplane scenario was real!

CHAPTER 9

THE MIRROR

The most obvious thing to scrutinize was my lifelong battle with my weight. It was my weight that made the statement and reflected back to me that I didn't really care for my body and mind the way I was "supposed to." So that became the groundbreaking focal point. I started to see that there were emotions underneath the pounds of flesh that I insulated myself with that needed to be addressed. I understood that living my life from anxiety attack to anxiety attack and never saying anything to anyone was going to get worse. And it did.

It made sense to start dissecting and inspecting my current belief systems, to start looking at every part of who I thought I was under a finely-focused lens. The problem I didn't see was that when you stare directly into the fire, you don't see anything else outside it. You don't see the things in your environment and relationships that add fuel to that fire. When you stand in your pain without the willingness to let go of it, you inevitably start to aim that pain at the people, places, and things around you. The brain's programming, like the anxiety that goes through the roof when you are emotionally triggered, becomes a reaction loop. Everything you say and do prompts and purposes the reaction loop. The anxiety is comfortable, recognizable, and justifiable.

My anxiety was a daily dose of fuel and was always something I kept to myself and fought through. I had watched and supported my mom through many anxiety and panic attacks when I was younger. When she froze in the driver's side of her Datsun and I had to lunge my leg over for the brake pedal and steer us to the shoulder, I learned to automatically separate myself from those moments of fear, pain, and any of the "extra" emotions that ensued. The post-partum depression after Bella's pregnancy was outside my fixed vision on the fire right in front of me and definitely added fuel. I had experienced it with two of my previous pregnancies and, regardless of knowing all the symptoms and the discussions with my OB, I didn't see it. Post-partum depression or not, it is quite literally impossible to see the whole picture while YOU are inside the frame.

When Bella was barely a week or so old, I had tried to go out to eat with Heath while we still had his stepmother staying with us, so we could grab some uninterrupted time to ourselves. In the restaurant, I experienced a horrible anxiety attack in front of him. I was overwhelmed by the people, the car ride there, leaving my newborn at home, and the thought of eating food or drinking something that might hurt my breastfeeding her. The walk to the bathroom to gather myself was too much too. And instead of explaining what was actually taking place, I lied. I lied to him after I lied to myself. I lied to myself because I believed I had to be OK and because I didn't want him or anyone else ever experiencing the massive fear that I grew up with. So, instead, I made it all about the baby and how it was too soon and how insensitive *he* was for trying to take me out of the house too soon. We got to-go containers for our freshly plated food, left my full Blue Moon sitting on the table, and drove home in utter silence, my eyeballs flooding tears and my nose spilling snot everywhere. I knew I had hurt him. I knew he was confused and angry. I knew I was confused at my behavior and angry at myself for not trusting him with me or me with me for that matter.

I never had the vulnerable conversations back then because I was afraid. Fear is easier to experience when it's masked by anger. Anger is easier to hold inside and easier to fire out at the nearest target, which often was my Love. The anger, frustration, confusion, betrayal, humiliation, and self-loathing was all just recycled and comingled inside my soul. I couldn't let go of it. It was a part of who I knew myself to be each day. I used it all to keep myself protected and far away from feeling. But it also kept me away from the very people I loved most.

Once we got home that afternoon, we continued to jab each other with barbed words, making the tension worse. Words that didn't really mean to come out of my mouth, let alone my heart, spewed angrily at him. That particular fight was a game-changer for me. I didn't recognize myself at all. It was almost like standing outside of myself. *That was not me. I'm not that angry, confused, hurt girl, lost and torn. I am his soul mate and best friend. Why am I hurting him at my own expense?*

Heath looked up at me from the bottom of the stairs, and the look I saw in his eyes completely gutted me. I knew that look. I had seen that look of anguish, disgust, betrayal, and soul-wrenching disappointment before, but not on him. I had seen it in front of a mirror years prior, in my previous marriage, where every day was about taking calculated guesses on whether today was a drinking day or not. My behaviors had become similarly abrasive and abusive to Heath now. This time, my self-loathing left no room for calculating moods. Instead, I was now a minefield, waiting for him to misstep.

That look was a look I didn't want to see in anyone's eyes ever again. Not in his, or (God forbid) in the eyes of my children. I was slowly breaking the heart of the man I loved most in this world, and he was letting me. I needed to grow beyond my pain, and I knew it. I needed to unpack my compartmentalized, safe little bags, and uncover all the lies residing in there, so I could truly experience my life and love myself. I needed to stand in my own power instead of my pain.

Hurt people hurt people. I didn't do what I had done on purpose, and that is what I told myself when I grasped what I was responsible for up to that day. What I didn't get at the time was in knowing that you are responsible, it also means you cannot ever "un-know" it. Every moment after that reflective reality was going to be purposeful for me. I had work to do, and it wasn't in the gym.

More often than not, we take the path of least resistance in the beginning of any change we make for ourselves. The changes we want and the changes we don't care for both create stress and an unsettling inside that we must learn to navigate. So, I started with what I really thought at the time was the problem: My life sucked because I was fat. If I could finally just get my weight and my eating under control, then he would be happy with me, I would be happy with me, and the kids would then be fine.

Let me just put it out there now. That is a lie we tell ourselves when we don't want to go below the surface, when we don't want to unpack a lifetime's supply of baggage, and actually let go of that lie. It's worth repeating: We all take that path of least resistance in the beginning. From the outside looking in, it was my ass that needed to move, not my mindset. So that is exactly what I did. That night after the breakdown and fight, as I peered down at Bella in my arms, swaddled and making scrunchy-baby-face-yawns, I whispered a promise in her ears. In one fell swoop that day, I had seen the many facets of myself, my life, my lies, all of which had been left unattended way too long. The little girl in my arms, the older kids in their beds, and the man who had stood earlier exasperated and in pain, needed me to come back to life as much as I did.

From that moment on, I had a responsibility to figure out why I had spent so many years trapped inside my own body, insulated by layers of pain, pancakes, late-night footlong subs, 2 a.m. Krumpe runs, and that ever-so-crisp layer of deep-fried self-loathing. No one was going to make it go away. No one was coming to fix it. I found that bottom that they talk about in all the AA meetings that I had walked my ex-husband to for years. Even that bump in the road was shining through with a purpose that I could finally identify—or was maybe more willing to finally see.

Bella was asleep, at last. I put the sleeping beauty down in her yellow bassinet, turned on the slow, soft music mode and picked up my cell phone to fix my life. That phone call was not the same as the one I made on my eighteenth birthday, when I was finally old enough to sign up for Jenny Craig and her overpriced, under-flavored, portion control—answers in a box. No, this time was different. This time would be it, for real.

That's still hard to fathom, that I have literally been trying to fix myself since my first double-digit birthday. I think back to all the birthday cakes that have been lit on fire between my tenth and thirty-third birthday, and shudder. I blew out those candles always wishing that my life would just get better and that the chocolate deliciousness would go to my boobs. I was an adorably cute little kid in my pink tights, bright blue leotard and scrunched up socks sticking out of Reebok pumps. I was prepared! That outfit was going to help me lose the chunk I avoided more and more as it took over me in the mirrors.

There was the ten-year-old me that followed Jane Fonda and Olivia Newton John. They were going to help me lose weight and learn to dance, too. If I dressed like them and I moved like them, I would eventually look like them. That would include the happiness that beamed on their faces in the VHS recordings in between jogging on a trampoline, leg-lift circles, and stair-stepper routines that I couldn't keep up with to save my life.

This was the beginning of my attempts to change myself on the outside, hiding away from myself on the inside and trying to present what I perceived others would be willing to accept. I memorized all the moves and even went so far as to transcribe the video for when I didn't have TV privileges.

It was around that same age that I started to own that how I felt and how I perceived my mirror image were very far apart from congruent. I did not like how I felt emotionally, but kept that separated from the "rest of me." I didn't like how I looked, but kept that in yet another "rest of me." At such a young age, I saw the first piece of disparity between my physical and emotional transformation. How many of us begin that separation of self and agree to turn a blind eye to each piece of ourselves?

We do what we do because it serves a purpose. I wanted to feel better about myself, and "self-esteem" was only an abstract concept that adults at school talked about, or that was in the Judy Blume books I got from the bookmobile. It took me writing out years later all the different ways I had tried to outsmart the fat factory, all the while lacquering on the extra layers through the years, to see it. I had made a pact with my then ten-year-old self that I would change the outside, and that would fix the inside of a little girl growing up, who was actually just trying to survive a really rough start in life.

At ten, I began the secret life of the yo-yo dieter. I drew out a calendar and tacked it to my wall behind my mirror so no one else knew it was there, and I marked stickers on the days I did my workout. The self-rewarding stickers turned into cheat days where I would have two servings at dinner instead of one, but only when no one was looking. I got good at inhaling my food so the second serving I stole looked like the first serving I had barely touched. The up-and-down of that cycle of reward and deprivation, the cravings for foods that were coming from the malnutrition I was imprisoning myself with and the excruciatingly emotional pain inside of me became "normal" to me. Add in the hormones that were kicking in and the lovely proclamation that announced "I am a woman now" at eleven years old, and I was just screwed. The battle of body versus brain had begun.

Living our life through the eyes of a scared ten-year-old little girl leads us to many dead ends. We grow our lies through cycles relentlessly repeated out of patterned habit that our brains run as programs by default. The pull and divide inside us begins when those cycles no longer serve a purpose. The limitations from the lies compound as we get older and our brains try over-zealously to remove the perceived pains, which even when healthy causes angst and change to the mind and body. The agreements I made at ten were still some of the agreements I was operating from in my thirties. This turned out as ineffective as it sounds, but I had to uncover the lies to rewrite them in a more effective—extraordinary way.

CHAPTER 10

MORE

Growing up in the silhouette of sorrow, surrounded by the pain, addiction, abuse, and the lies that threaded them all together, is a marathon event. It is not an overnight process to recovery. The lies became agreements I chose to carry with me. At the age of fourteen, I saw a commercial for Dexatrim. I figured out that buying it on the weekends when my Uncle Bob came to take us to the mall would be the opportune time. I took them out of the packaging and popped each of them out of their little bubble and put them in an ibuprofen container I kept in my purse. When I was fifteen, I found a Suzanne Somers Thigh Master at a yard sale in my development. I used my allowance on that, because making those thighs burn was going to attack the weight of emotional pain that was continuing to grow inside my soul. I was a size 16 by that time. Not too bad looking back on it, but it was catastrophic through my teenage eyes.

By the time I turned sixteen, I was up yet another two sizes. I made additional agreements with myself to get rid of the shame, embarrassment, and lack of control in my own life. I continued the search for something to change me. I saw a woman on a late-night paid commercial that was literally screaming about being able to see a gap between her thighs for the first time in her whole life, and I related. I understood what she called "the insanity." As she stomped out onto the stage in front of hundreds of people in her belted sweatpants, scrunchy socks, and her crop top with the neck cut out, something resonated inside me. She was speaking words that actually made sense!

I was ready when she asked if we were finally ready to stop, because I was living in that insanity. I contemplated making myself throw up, but it grossed me out to see my food twice like that, so that was a no-go. I also began the starvation-deprivation diet. That carried me through my junior and senior year of high school. I remember thinking then that if I only had a Snickers and a Dr Pepper for breakfast, and stuck to the salad bar at lunch, and then had one serving at dinner, I would finally begin to see the change I wanted to see in my body. I thought that I would finally start to notice a difference in my moods. My friendships would increase, my grades would go back up, my family life would get better, and I would feel happy, just like everyone else.

The un-released lie of my high school-self, that everything was going to be OK and I just had to persevere through it stoically, was nothing more than the egotistical mindset of my ten-year-old self, I could see things weren't as they appeared. But I was also emotionally stunted by my upbringing. We must know that we cannot judge yesterday's decisions using today's knowledge nor can we forgive ourselves until we are ready to choose forgiveness over the pain holding us hostage. I learned this through my journey as I began to desire more opportunities to tell the truth. That truth took many years to illuminate itself. But awakening to it allowed me to start living my life free of pain on purpose.

After watching that program, I started to slowly accept that I really couldn't keep living my life that way anymore. I was a smart girl. I was on honor roll and in AP classes, college-bound and career-track ready. But even though something had to change, I didn't know what or how. This knowledge didn't stop me from pursuing my life with my ten-year-old little girl's agreements and lies running the show, all decked out in her *Jem and the Holograms* costume. I was going to keep on keeping on until something stopped me.

Realizing that the tiny prepackaging of portion-controlled options was not going to work, I also was heading towards a new life adventure of first-time motherhood. I experienced my first round of the "Screw it; I can eat for two" attitude. That carried me through kids one through three when I again thought that the problem to solve was my weight. There's nothing quite like beating a dead horse. In my mind, it had nothing at all to do with the severely alcoholic man beating me, raping me physically and emotionally, nor the three children all under the age of five. It was not the overwhelm that came with navigating the welfare system, the childcare vouchers, or the employment I was required to find unless I went back to school. It most definitely had nothing to do with the fact that I no longer had any ties with my own family at all and was completely isolated in a state with no game plan, no hope, and a ten-year-old's operating system that by this time had her heart broken so many times "feeling better" or looking better was the least of my problems. It was definitely just my waist size that was ruining my life and about to destroy my future and my children's future. That was the loudest lie I told myself. All that chaos was OK and I had to just survive it. All my extra weight was an excess of pain, not pounds. And no matter how good I got at carrying it or covering it up, I was still lying.

Immersing myself in my studies somewhat protected me growing up, and academics had become my world again by the time I had my first daughter, my third child. I was the most *me* when I was in class, researching, or writing a paper. It felt good and natural to go back to school. I tried to apply it to my life outside of school and decided all I needed was to research how to live a happy, healthy life. I just needed instructions on how to make my life better. My husband, at the time, needed a center to give him instructions to get better. I found Herbalife; he found a month-long rehab program. All the pills and shakes I drank religiously at exact time intervals worked for a while. I was extremely disciplined and committed. The weight began to come off, Jesse was away and working on himself, and I began to feel good inside. My ten-year-old-self perceived that the pills and dieting healed me, not the break from the daily stress and violence. So when the weight came back on after my husband returned from rehab, I turned to stronger pills.

Metabolife completely eliminated my appetite and gave me the energy to buzz around (and off the walls) for days. The appetite suppressants were the perfect-sized bandages on the gaping hole inside. I was starving for love, acceptance, and self-awareness. I just kept feeding myself in hopes that something would stick to my physical and emotional ribs!

With each new strategy, including this pill, I truly believed I had finally figured it out! When you aren't hungry, you don't eat. When you don't eat, you lose weight. You also lose your mind, overwork the heart, and wind up in the emergency room. I sat outside my oldest son's elementary school, waiting to pick him up from his first day of kindergarten, when I found myself experiencing heart palpitations. I thought they would pass after my son got in the car, but they didn't let up. I had to pull over after leaving the drop circle to call 911. Definitely not one of my finest moments. The doctors explained to me, "No, you did not and are not having a heart attack, but you did take something that is no longer on the shelves for a reason."

The correlation between food-hungry and life-hungry started to grow stronger inside of me with each day. I mentioned before how "smart a woman I know I am." I was definitely not going to buy anything over-the-counter ever again. It didn't work at fourteen, and it almost killed me in my twenties. So I went to the doctor for help. I walked out of the doctor's office with a three-month prescription of phentermine. It was not as effective as Metabolife, but I did notice a difference. I continued using that until I found out I was pregnant with my fourth child. I began the "eating-for-two syndrome" again through the rest of my pregnancies. It was so much easier to retreat inside myself and pretend I was accepting defeat, that this was just me. I told myself that being big-boned and heavier was OK. I started to rationalize how much happier I would be if I could just accept my size.

This was me, the sum of all my parts, albeit frustrated and frayed at the edges, but it was me, and those were my parts! There had to be more than this! This woman, unhappily married, with all these kids, unfinished degrees, unemployed, overweight, and overwhelmed… This was "just me?!" I wanted more than that. I knew somewhere inside of myself that there was more than that but where, how, and why, still eluded me.

CHAPTER 11

TIPPING THE SCALES

It took me until Seven of Nine was a few months old and several conversations with my current husband, Heath, before we started doing an exercise program I ordered. We did P90X every single night at about 8:30 PM. There was so much already on our plates, and in some respects, this was just one more thing to do. It was also cripplingly hard! I have been a coach for the Beachbody programming for ten years, and I still won't recommend that program jumping out the gate.

Heath drove a truck and jumped in and up and out and down about five hundred times a day. That person who drives the giant one-arm trucks, running up one side and down the other to carry away your recycling, that was my guy for over eleven years. My husband worked ten- to twelve-hour shifts, and the last thing he wanted to do was move more, on purpose no less.

He hated that job. I hated that job for him. It kept him trapped and alone, but it played a huge part in saving our marriage during my years of mental and emotional absence. I know he did it for me. I know without any doubt at all that he came home after all those horribly long days in the heat and the cold and rain and stood next to me jumping, cussing, and dying so I would move out of the space I believed I was stuck in. My husband was always that kind of man. He'd give you the shirt right off his back, sit and listen to you for days, and have a laundry list of prioritized options, all completely viable. His job kept him sane amongst the insanity. To go from zero kids to insta-dad of five took moxie. He never wavered in front of them, and not very often in front of me. He spent every waking hour cultivating a safe home for us all to be a family in together (and I'd swear he did so in his sleep too).

When he started coming home and working out with me, I felt both elated and extremely guilty. It was a struggle to stay out of my own way and accept the support and compassion being given each day. My trauma-based brain wanted to know when it would all stop and blow up in my face. But I held my breath instead of speaking my truth or identifying my fears for what they were.

We had a great routine. We took turns showering afterwards, getting the baby down, and putting the other six kids to bed for the night. We did it for ninety days and I lost my first fifty pounds. I felt physically phenomenal! But I still battled the feelings of numbness in my mind. I felt juxtaposed. We had begun to bond again, and the tension between us started to let up easily. I even liked what it felt like to have him look at me "that way" again after so long. Slowly, a light beamed through, full of hope that I could have more.

That feeling didn't stick, though. It scared me. What does a foodie do when she is scared? She eats! What does she do when she's happy? She eats more. What does she do when she's not happy? She unhinges her jaw and with both arms, pulls everything towards her, and inhales deeply. I saw where this was headed and decided to really focus on being consistent. I consistently lasted a few days at a time. I was able to hold onto the drive I had found and what I wanted, but I let my weight creep back on and I was starting to feel those oh-so-comfortable feelings of misery and doubt again. I had almost doubted my way all the way back up to where I started from before I drew the line in the proverbial sand. The weight had come off me physically, but the emotional anchor weighing down my daily decisions had not budged. I still struggled with intimacy, vulnerability, and having an open and unconditional line of communication with my husband. My children were growing in some type of warp-speed universe that kept me counting down how many years I had left with them instead of looking forward to how many years my new-found health was going to give us. There was an unspoken urgency inside me as I ran to and from an imaginary timeline that I truly believed was going to run out for me and my opportunity to be.

Tipping the scales towards three hundred again was not an option! I did another round of the seemingly self-torturing program. It kicked my ass and shrunk it again, thank heavens! I ate better this time, and it started to stick. I was slowly understanding that I did have control over my own body and mind and that my heart didn't have to hurt all the time. I adopted a mindset of consistently showing up for myself each day. This second round of self-inflicted burpees was behavior-busting! I saw the connection between moving my body and moving my mind. It felt good to feel good. The feeling was infectious. I wanted more. The connection between feeding my body and fueling my body to improve my physical health was laying foundational pieces of my framework. I was healing my body and making room in my heart. I wanted more.

The conversations with Heath began to get longer and deeper into the traumas I had underwent and what he had been experiencing all these years after them by my side. Finding my health again gave me the strength to try harder in our marriage. In the beginning of it all, I had started a journal as a tool to check in and have accountability. I had this fantasy that I would fill it with all the days ahead, sharing my journey and the struggles along the way so one day someone would be able to look at what I used to look like and who I used to be and know they too could do it. I was slowly creating the proof that I was worth the effort. Some of the agreements I had made all those years ago were starting to soften, making room for more. The lie that I was a failure was finally being laid to rest.

But it was much more than just feeling better about how I looked. My outside was changing, but I still perceived my life through the eyes of a stagnant ten-year-old girl. Just like that little girl I was, I had turned to food for comfort and become overweight, overwhelmed, and eventually trapped inside my own mind and body. My weight-loss adventure became more about finding out who I was and reconnecting with myself than about being skinny. One of my sons struggled with all my same food behaviors, and I needed to be able to teach him—and all my children—that healthy was an option that could include happiness. I had to learn for myself that the success of a person is measured by who they are, not by the failure to be who they were supposed to be. This one was difficult to navigate at times, more so than others. I had so many poor beliefs still within me about what I should have been doing and who I should've turned out to be. I had bags to unpack and lies to let go.

CHAPTER 12

OWN THY SELF

When we change, the people closest to us are often-times thrown for a loop. The realization that I have never truly been *me* in my marriage made it difficult to be close to my husband. I needed and wanted the support he had been giving me for years, but I was not the same woman he had been giving it to. That created a distance between us that was difficult to discern. In many ways, we had to learn each other all over again for the first time. It was like having to completely start over in many ways. I didn't want it to be that way, and neither did he.

After one argument, Heath told me, "I don't know who you are anymore." That's one of the most heart-wrenching sentences to hear from the man you share life with. He was right, though. That understanding was excruciating for me and for him. We have been through so much over the years together that to sit side-by-side and contemplate a divorce neither of us believed in our hearts would solve anything was agonizing.

But through those conversations, he gave me a gift. I was afforded the opportunity to release another lie and make room for love, gratitude, and joy. The old lie that said, "I'm not worth loving, and every relationship that means something to me ends this way" was just that: a lie. I didn't have to stay in this relationship the way it was. I could choose to grow from this moment with him and see it as an opportunity for both of us. It didn't mean that everything was over. All the changes I had experienced through my years of learning to wake up and live my life more presently had given him more of a woman to love and live this life with. I was just getting to know her myself; how could I expect him to know her?

I was not a victim in this relationship, and it was time to stop acting like one. Taking control of how I treated my body, learning to love myself again, and valuing myself for the first time, allowed us to embark on renewing our vows to each other. It also gave me another chance to be the mom I actually wanted to be with all my children. The more I laid claim to myself and actively sought to understand how I got to be this woman, the more significant I began to realize that I was in my own life.

At this point in the story, I have diligently kept my midnight promise to my then one-week old. I have lost over one hundred pounds and gained an entire new perspective on my life and experiences. My husband was beginning his own adventures with learning more about himself and how to unpack his bags, and our children were beginning to flourish and grow as well in light of our journey.

What we had done together was turning out to be very pivotal for my home life and my health. I was beginning to see how living life on purpose alleviated my anxiety. When you purposefully intend to do something, it takes the regret and sorrow out of the equation and builds up your emotional integrity. I applied this concept to my exercises by scheduling them and making sure I showed up for myself. Consistently showing up in my life led me to developing what would soon be my three-step process to FitMinded Living. I now ate with intention and noticed that I enjoyed my foods more and ate less at each meal, without starving or feeling like I was losing my mind. I didn't feel the deprivation most diets triggered in me, and I didn't feel the overwhelm that used to come from following the routine schedule of an exercise program. I enjoyed them. I noticed my mind clearing up and my emotions evening out. I talked more about my feelings and felt more present with each moment.

I understood first-hand what it means to start from our own beginning and that the journey is meant to be individual and intimate. Heath and I shared with one another how we walked this path and what we unpacked from our bags along the way, but the work we each did was ours individually. That differentiation can get glossed over in relationships pretty easily. It happens when we have a life full of "supposed to's" instead of accepting what "is" in each moment.

When we over-extend ourselves, doing things for other people, it doesn't leave us time to examine what we need or the room to see the lies needing to be shed. That over-extension happens when we let the kids, the job, the sports, and everything else under the sun stand between us and the life we say we want to experience. For Heath and me, there was a time we literally had five different baseball teams going with the kids. We were completely outnumbered and over-extended in every way possible, but we held onto our belief that each of them was going to have a greater life because of our willingness to endure.

"I have to suffer so others can have what I want for them and what I can't have for myself." That is another lie we tell ourselves. Your suffering heals no one. It does keep you justified in your pain and angst. It also keeps you protected from experiencing vulnerability and pushes those you love most further away. But not only that, it keeps you so busy that it hinders you from digging up those lies you've buried deep inside you. It only serves to perpetuate the cycle of lies and keep you trapped comfortably with them.

Do you want to get out of there? Then let's start talking about how to break free.

CHAPTER 13

NO FEAR

Let's dive into how I met this incredible man I'm married to today. It's a great story, one of my favorites! Years ago, during my junior year, I walked into my Environmental Science classroom situated in the back of Middletown High School and took my seat next to my best friend. As we giggled and wondered who would be joining us at our table, in walked a boy with dirty blond hair and blue eyes that from the very moment I saw them, I knew my heart belonged to him. In the short time it took for me to catch my breath, I knew my life would be amazing with him, though I didn't even know his name. His stunning blue eyes and his purposeful silence caught my attention. But his black baseball cap really stood out to me. The phrase "No Fear" lined the top of his cap.

The whimsical fairytale that I felt and lived out in that brief moment, where all I got was literally a smirk across his face when I said hello, would sustain a piece of my heart for years that I would not reclaim until we were much older. Neither one of us had any idea of what was waiting ahead and if we had, we both agree, we would allow it to play out the very same way.

I was ecstatic to go to a science class I detested, just so I could see this mysterious boy, who I later learned, was named Heath. I wanted to know everything about him. He was so quiet, but when he did talk, his words were piercing. Every comment was laced with dry sarcasm that was easy to take personally, until that smile gave him away. His smile was in his eyes, and it would peek out behind the turmoil that I could see in them so clearly. It was like we knew each other already, even though we'd just met for the first time. We became fast friends and enjoyed each other's company daily.

Heath began picking me up before school and we would drive in together. Toad the Wet Sprocket songs would blare when I got in and took my seat. I would sit in the passenger side, praying that the car would jerk just enough to give me just cause to grab his hand or he mine. Every morning and afternoon, it felt like I was encapsulated safely inside the most amazing bubble with someone I had a seventeen-year-old's crush on, but also was falling truly in love with. The more time that went on, we began to talk on the phone for hours each night. One night, we talked from the moment he got home from his restaurant job until the moment it was time to go to school. Little did we know the foreshadowing of that night and how it would play out ten years later across the country.

I didn't tell many people about the depression my mother suffered or the abuse that we all sustained at home. That was another lie I got good at telling. If no one knew what my home life was like, then they couldn't judge me for it. The school counselors knew my family, as did the support staff, and a few teachers that found me in tears when my mother kicked me out of the house during one of her episodes. There were not many around me who knew that the only safe hours in the day for me existed inside the Middletown High School walls.

By the time I had met this young boy and started experiencing aspects of myself that I could not allow out, it was too late. My heart was head over heels and my soul had been imprinted upon. It had not been my home that he was picking me up from every morning. It was the home of a lady who went to church with my best friend's parents. She had heard about my circumstances and wanted to help. The amazing part, to me, was that I knew both her daughters and had met them one of the times I was allowed to attend the church services with my friend.

So, I was sharing the bedroom of another sixteen-year-old girl's home. She and her sister, both welcomed me, no questions asked. But I felt awkward and displaced. The family never made me feel excluded, but I did not know how to *feel* included in a family any more than I knew how to *feel* close to this young boy I was falling deeper and deeper in love with.

Little by little, I began giving him pieces of my story, trying also to keep my own level of embarrassment to a minimum. He never judged me. He never ran away from me. As I got to know him, though, he had his own bags of unpacked traumas, as well. The cosmic plan unveiling itself at the time is much more obvious now than it was back then. Our paths crossed as young teenagers just long enough for us both to experience what it felt like to be honest and true with another person, and then it was over.

The one and only kiss he planted on my face was one I held deep inside my heart until I saw him again ten years later.

I still had not disclosed why I was living with another family, nor had I spoke of my mother, sister, brother, or my step-father. I wanted to keep them and that reality a secret from this perfect person in my world. Our senior year at Middletown was starting. I had finally felt like a real, live girl, with friends, a best friend who happened to finally be a boy, and a mom and sisters who unofficially adopted me. I had a family I was proud to be a part of and a life that felt like it was worth living. Still, there were spells when my heart ached for my brother and sister. I could only see them when they were in school. It wrenched my heart that they were forbidden to talk to me or that they would be punished at home if they did so. My brother and I would sneak time before he got on the bus after school or he would "miss" the bus on accident. Our mother caught on to that rather quickly, though. My sister, still in middle school, was not able to do the same, so phone calls happened but only when she could sneak the phone out of our mother's locked bedroom door.

Our mother kept everything locked. Her bedroom, the front door, the back door, the bathroom door, too. We were allowed to enter the bathroom from the hallway entrance, but not the kitchen side, as that was hers. The windows were always covered, and the lights turned out for the most part. She kept us in her darkness, as if she wanted us to experience what was going on in her mind. There was a tall, brown, double-door pantry cabinet in the kitchen with a lock that only she had the key to. She kept the key on a wrist-sized silver ring around her tiny arm. The only time it came off was when she placed it on the nightstand beside her bed or in the bathroom. She kept herself and her keys locked safely in one wing of our house. She had made a living space on one side and a bedroom on the other. My step-father had his own room and a card table in front of his TV downstairs in the basement. That had a lock on it, too. She could lock him down there and he would use the garage as access into and out of his tiny space. Looking back, I understand why small appliances started coming into the house. They were for him to still be able to eat! Her food was kept in that big brown pantry. All her toiletries and possessions were under lock and key.

Slowly my house was sectioned off as we grew older and farther away from each other. It often felt like that if she could have had smaller pantries for each of us, she would have kept us under lock and key, too. Our house was not a home; it was a giant pantry with doors she would lock and unlock with the wave of her moods. It was imperative that when a down-spiral struck that each of us was on the inside of that locking door or we would be denied access to the bare necessities, even our bed to sleep in at night. We were all locked out of so many aspects of her, and as we grew older, she tried valiantly to lock us away from the world with her.

I know it was not on purpose, but to a teenage girl who had been covering the mommy role for the other two kids in the house, it was beyond stifling. She was unable to function out in the real world, even when that real world was only a trip to the grocery store or to Thom McAnn for direly needed shoes. The only way she could keep us was if we stayed inside her ever-shrinking and faster-closing pantry doors. She tried to keep us at a safe distance to protect us from the pain she wasn't dealing with, but it spilled over onto all of us and kept a tight hold on to each of us for years. This behavior stemmed out of her own childhood and marital traumas, and it was a pattern I unfortunately learned as well and continued in my own marriages.

The depressive spells were just long-lasting bad moods to us when we were little. Some were explosive, and others were reclusive. Mom had days where she just wouldn't come out. She would wake when we came home from school and go to sleep when we were supposed to be getting up and ready for the day. She did not work a night job; she just could not sleep when the rest of the house was silent. She would spend nights trying to make up for the rest of what she was not doing for us as a parent, like making special breakfasts of pancake-covered sausage links in the Snackmaster. I knew it was an especially bad night for her when those tasty treats were in the fridge, with paper-plate name tags on them for each of us and a smiley face with her acknowledgment that she did, indeed, love us.

There were many nights as a young girl I would purposefully stay awake until the wee hours of the morning, when she was in her best moods, so I could talk with her or show her I could be a good girl. So many of our conversations were strained and pressured as she just didn't know what to say or do with a growing girl or the two kids following behind me. She didn't know how to get out of the second abusive relationship that she ran into to escape my father, and she had no one to turn to anymore. Looking back, I can understand the life-stunting happenstances that took place for this woman, and that willingness to accept who she was forced me to accept who I was. She became pregnant with me at fifteen years old and ran away with her sister's fiancé to get married. The "favorite child" had become the household whore, and I was the fruitful accident. This became a theme replayed when I turned fifteen. My mother's fear that I would befall the same horrors that she did underlined and interfered with every authentic moment possible between a mother and her once adored child.

The first time my mother sent me away, I was two years old. It was a safety measure so my brother, who was just born, and I would be safe from the beatings my mother went through on a daily basis. My father physically, mentally, and sexually abused a then seventeen-year-old girl—my mother. Through both her pregnancies, the abuse grew worse and more volatile. When I was seven months inside her, she was flung down a flight of stairs and left to get herself to the hospital. She was sodomized by a man who professed undying love to her and yet he was still the better of the two evils in her life. When I was two years old, my father, the man who abused my mother religiously, accidentally dislocated my right shoulder from its socket when he was yanking me out of my grandmother's arms. I was his property, too.

Despite this ownership of me, he pretty much stayed out of my life after my mom left him for my step-father.

No child support, no nothing. When I was eight years old, my mom had to stage a SWAT-style arrest for my pretend kidnapping to get the $30,000 he owed her. That was the last time I saw him before I met Jesse.

As a child, I learned to just wait it out. Whatever it was, whomever it was, I had to just wait, be still, and be quiet. Away from everyone, I had many words, many tantrums, many tears, and many breakdowns, but never an actual say in how my life went down. Another lie formed: "I am not in control and have no say over my life or the people in it." As a young adult of sixteen and seventeen, I started to speak up more. As I grew older and was allowed more legal room to live a "real" life, I also began to disassemble inside. I was resilient when it came to trauma and stress, but had very little clue as to the real-life ramifications of my still immature actions, decisions, and behaviors. Also in that line up of unknowns was the teenage desire to be a real, grown-up girl with real, grown-up girl qualities and experiences; those envisioned by the teenage mindset and all her crucial moments: a sweet sixteen party, a best friend, a first kiss.

All the while, this surreal, you-can't-make-this-shit-up type of life kept rolling around me, I was trying to literally just survive it. And in the middle of it all, this amazing young boy who made every moment a butterflies-in-the-tummy moment, was becoming more intriguing and more difficult to be with at the same time. I didn't have to keep all my history a secret from him anymore, and he did accept what I divulged, but my own insecurities ate at me. My lack of experiences with the social norms of being a teenager impeded my ability to be one. The newfound freedoms I discovered, along with the tight friendship this boy and I had formed, were intoxicating, overwhelming, and paralyzing. The love that he gentlemanly turned down was eating at me as well. I didn't understand why he didn't want to move forward beyond a friendship, and I assumed I was the problem. In the years since we have been married, Heath shared how much he respected me and our friendship. His forethought at such a young age actually gave us both the room to find ourselves and our friendship again years later. The foundation we had put in place in the face of teenage fears and uncertainty stayed strong and weathered trauma and time.

During the year and half that we had been getting to know each other I had also been getting to know my father again. I was a janitorial assistant for the high school that year. After school I would clean the classrooms for three of my favorite teachers. The classrooms had telephones in them and back then you just called 411 to get the number for someone you wanted to call. There were 34 listings for my last name in the state of New Mexico where my parents had fled to elope. My father's family all lived there. After about three weeks of slowly running down the list of prospective candidates, I finally found the right Tolbert to which I said over the phone, "Hi, I think I'm your daughter." He immediately said my name back to me followed with, "I knew you'd find me."

Some time after that, I went out to visit my father for the first time since the faked kidnapping when I was eight years old. It was out there that I met Jesse while I was out to breakfast. I fell hard for this exciting new man that played heavy metal, wore a black leather jacket, loved baking, and taking me all over the New Mexico terrain. It wasn't a hard decision to move out to New Mexico with him. After my failed college attempt, I had no real ties to hold me back. Still heartbroken with the teenage angst of unrequited love and feeling lost in my life, the prospect of an enormous door closing behind me and the possibility of one opening was exactly what I wanted and needed. And it was just so immensely different. I was game for the head first plunge into the unknown and the maybe, might be of come what may. It was the perfect opportunity to start my life fresh. It was also the picturesque epitome of running away from oneself at full speed.

Before I moved across the country with Jesse, I went through the Kenny Rogers Roasters drive-thru where he worked, one last time, in hopes I'd see him again before I started the next chapter in my crazy life. In my head that day, I played out a hundred different scenarios. I contemplated telling him the truth… *"Hi, I know it's been months since we last talked or saw each other. But I really am still in love with you and I think you are in love with me, too, but you are too scared to try. So, before I leave for Albuquerque with a guy I met while visiting my father after not seeing him since I was eight, I wanted to give you this last chance to come to your senses, realize you love me, and that we are supposed to live happily ever after…".*

I went ahead and pulled up to not order anything from him at all and smiled and said, "Hi! I am moving to New Mexico this weekend and just wanted to say goodbye."

He said, "That's awesome, good luck." I pulled out of that drive-thru with my heart splintered in a million pieces and cried a thousand silent tears over a love I knew in my bones was real.

Both of us went on to marry and go our separate ways. The intimate moments we shared, and those we did not, haunted my soul. And yet, they protected the most innocent part of me through the next ten years of trauma, turmoil, and a path only a life of preset destiny or serendipity could navigate us through. Neither of us knew our paths would ever cross again.

CHAPTER 14

FAT-FREE REALITY BITES

The truth is, I knew I shouldn't have left for New Mexico with Jesse. I knew I was running full speed ahead with my lies, away from everyone that knew me. I was too scared to be vulnerable and honest with myself. I wasn't willing to accept myself or grow from that spot, either. The buzz of the busyness, that false sense of the progress we feel when we move full-speed ahead, actually equates to being empty.

That busyness is a distraction from working through your own pain. By involving yourself in so much activity, you may think you're filling your life with fulfilling things. But filling your calendar doesn't always translate to a full life. Think of it like a fat-free dessert. It looks the same as the real stuff, might even taste the same. But when you break down what it's made of, it's full of empty calories with little to no nutritional value. That's where I was in my journey to Albuquerque. My life was about to be chock-full of fat-free everything and not just as a means of weight loss.

It would be ten years down the road before the next conversation with the man I knew I was meant to walk my last steps with in this life would take place. This reunion was divinely aligned and right on time. But first, there would be the happenstances that brought us back together.

I was standing in my living room on the top step headed towards my bedroom in New Mexico and the phone rang in my hand. It was a Maryland number—my Uncle Bob's house number—my heart smiled and I quickly answered it. I was excited to talk to the man who had made my life make sense every time he was in it. When I was little, he was my whole world. Every morning I got to spend at my grandmother's corner kitchen table with him, eating kielbasa and scrambled Egg Beaters, was like sitting with Super Man. He always smelled of fresh-brewed coffee and aftershave. I still love those smells and smile inside when it wafts past my nose.

I loved giving him kisses on his cheek. The rough-scruff of the I-shaved-but-it's-been-a-few-hours always tickled my lips and cheek as I dove in for the biggest hug in the world from him before he left to go to work. His hugs were the type of hugs that made me feel like I was still a little girl of five years old inside, no matter how tall I kept getting. I always felt like he would be here forever, and I would often tell him so. With that same inside smile, I answered the phone, and waited to hear his slow drawl saying, "Tina Darlin', hello."

Instead of his warm familiar voice, I heard the very abrupt voice of his common-law wife, Terry, on the other end of the phone, telling me she was fulfilling her promise to me. Terry wasn't really my aunt, per se, just the lady that had shared life with Uncle Bob for years. He wasn't ever interested in marrying. Terry was just there at all the functions that he was at one day and kept being there.

Before I moved to Albuquerque, I went to dinner at the Red Horse Inn and had a delicious steak dinner with her and the man who had been a father to me. That turned out to be the very last time I saw him. When he and I hugged, he promised to always love me no matter where life took me. When we hugged goodbye, Terry promised to let me know if anything ever happened. The phone in my hand started making a noise I couldn't understand while my heart jumped from my chest. The words came across the phone line, but they did not register in my mind. I tried to ask why and what, but her words didn't reach me any more than the blood I needed to circulate my brain. But I tried to utter some semblance of words to form the questions attacking my mind.

She explained that he had not only died of pancreatic cancer, but he had already been laid to rest in his home-town of Staunton, Virginia, a month ago. "His will is being contested," she said. "We need you and your mother to come to the court proceedings." The floor beneath me gave way as my legs buckled and my left arm reached out to catch my fall. I fought the impulse to throw my phone at the bedroom wall. I was drowning in the tears of incomprehension and in anger as this family-fracturing arrest of my soul flooded through me. All I could see was my reflection in the mirror on the wall showing a grown woman half-lying on the floor clutching her heart and pounding the floor beneath her, needing to be held and comforted by something, someone.

As Terry relayed how many months Uncle Bob had been in the hospital dying, all I could do was sit on the floor and hug myself, alone and oblivious to the five children running outside the bedroom door. Jesse was still not home from yet another bender. Inside, I seethed with questions. How could she not call me when he went into the hospital? How could not one person pick up the damn phone and tell me the man who had loved me like a daughter and healed every broken piece of my heart grow- ing up, was dying? Then the next onslaught of questions blasted my brain. How the hell could *he* not tell me? Why did he not ask for me?

I remember that last call from him, and he sounded like his normal I'm-getting-older-self. We exchanged the same "You will be here forever" statement that I always truly meant. He had known differently, and he didn't let on at all. It has taken me years to find my solace within that devastation, but I hold to the knowledge that I will forever remember him as the Super Man at Grandma's kitchen table, as the tall, strong, gentle man who made me golf left-handed so I could "expand my brain," as the man who incessantly sang Christmas songs in July with the voice of Frank Sinatra. I will never know what the illness did to him, and I know that is how he wanted it to be for me.

That was the beginning of a very long night and what turned out to be the beginning of a life-changing event. I had to call my mother that night after I pulled myself together, as no one had told her of his passing, either. I could hear her frail body hit the floor even ten states away. The phone dropped from her hand, and I listened to her sob for what seemed like eternity. I couldn't hang up the line. I wasn't going to leave her alone in it like I had been. I told her I was catching the next flight from Albuquerque and before I closed my eyes that night, I had booked my flight and only had to figure out who would be able to take care of the kids while I was gone.

The next morning as I sat up in my still half-empty bed, I wrestled with the hole inside my heart and the searing anger that (yet again) the man who was supposed to be there for me was out there, somewhere, sleeping off his latest blackout. As I got the kids dressed, I remembered every birthday that Uncle Bob never forgot, even though he had not got to meet any of his grand-nieces and nephews. He was the first one to send a birthday card that always included a twenty-dollar bill to "buy your precious something sweet." Then the realities started to flood in one by one. He wasn't going to meet them ever. He would never get to hold the sweet little boy who would carry on his name, or tell me how much my girls reminded him of me when I was little.

I wrestled in my soul to fight the surrounding proofs that, yet again, I was insignificant. Who treats another human being like this? Where was the love, compassion, kindness? Why was my life seemingly submerged in pain, anger, familial vendettas, and utter disregard for one another? How was this what I was willingly staying in? How was this what I was raising my own children to accept as "normal?" These were just some of the questions that would bounce around in my mind for years. Learning to unravel my own role and responsibility in upholding that way of living led me to uncovering the parts of me that were hiding away, held in place by every single lie.

The next time the phone hit my ear, it was to call and talk to the grown-up boy I had loved so many moons ago. He shockingly had answered my whimsical let's-see-what-happens email from months prior that I had sent through classmates.com. At that time in my life, I knew my marriage was coming to an end. In the ending of something, though, there is always a beginning. I was slowly finding pieces of myself again with each friend from years past and there was a drive inside me growing again…to live again…away from all the pain and anguish and guilt that enveloped me while I was surrounded by the violence, booze, and throat punches.

Heath and I had been talking almost daily by this time. I would sit in the car-wash bay next to the daycare center that I ran, with my Bluetooth tucked into my ear and arms curled happily around my knees as I teeter-tottered back and forth. I felt like I was seventeen all over again, smiling through our catch-up conversations. This particular morning, through weepy words, I explained that I had to come back to Maryland to be with my mother and attend court proceedings for my uncle's estate. We talked about what I wanted to do there after not being back for so many years and how I would be bringing my youngest son with me.

As we discussed possible hotels and places to rent cars, he exclaimed "Duh, I have an extra room you two can use, and it's free!" I laughed, thinking he was joking. "No, I'm serious," he said. "I don't mind at all." Even in the wake of the horror of what had happened, there was a knowing voice inside me that screamed, "YES!" Things were starting to shift for the better.

CHAPTER 15

CHICKIE

A few days later, a dirty-blond, curly-haired, three-year-old bounced on my knees in the back of the plane while we waited for take-off. I remembered how much I hated flying. Leaving the ground at sky-rocket speed, facing straight upward, watching the ground become a multi-colored blur, and my stomach always taking an immediate flight of its own straight up to my throat makes the whole thing kind of nauseating. As a mom, though, you can't really sit too long in those moments, especially while your toddler is looking around in amazement, thinking this is the coolest ride ever.

Justin always looked at everything with the widest blue eyes that held silent inquisition and merriment. His blue eyes were just like his father's, kind of like a stormy blue sky. Justin was a lot like me, even then. He never let anyone know that he afraid of anything. Not even the loud, thundering engines of the plane were going to shake him. I wondered that morning if the roar of all the fights that took place in our home fell on the same seemingly fearless ears. I wondered if he was able to tune us out in much the same way he tuned out the engines roaring in our ears. I hoped he did.

I stepped outside myself that morning while seated in the sardine box with wings and inhaled the stale air blow-ing fast and straight at my face from above. I reflected on last week's mega-fight. I had class after work that day. So, I left the kids at day-care instead of taking them home to be with Jesse. It was best for them, and it gave me a sense of security while I was away working on my someday-degree. That morning had started at 5 a.m. getting the kids and myself ready and dressed while Jesse slept off his hangover. I happily walked out of the house leaving that crap behind me and locking it in the house. I called to check on him at lunchtime to make sure he was at least up and out of bed. I reminded him that I had classes that night and wouldn't be home until late. He tried to convince me that it was OK if I dropped the kids off before class, or that he could pick them up and bring them home. I argued that he needed to take this down time for himself and just leave the kids to go on that evening's field trip to Peter Piper. He begrudgingly agreed and said he would hang out with his mom and sister then. That was code for "F- you, then. I will go to the Circle K convenience store, buy my fifth of Evan Williams, and check out until some time tomorrow." *Nothing new there,* I thought. *Maybe he won't come home at all and I can get on with my life and start enjoying my children.*

When I parked in the driveway of our Golden Gate Drive home that night, I didn't want to get out of my van. I wanted to quietly, stealth-like, put it slowly in reverse, back out, and just drive with no destination in mind other than *away*. I wanted away from all of this. This couldn't be what my life amounted to after so many years. I remember thinking, *I'm twenty-seven years old and still taking part-time classes at a junior college to try to get my associate's, working fifty hours a week at a day care so I can keep my children with me all day when they are not in school to keep them out of the house, and not wanting to pull into the driveway of my own home? I am completely dependent on food stamps, section 8 housing, state medical insurance, and a job that barely puts food on the table or gas in my van, while he sits at home pretending to fix appliances and drinks half of my paycheck. I am afraid to stop any of it or turn to someone for help because I don't want them to take my children away from me. I am afraid of all the assumptions they will make about who I am or who I'm not.*

There were more days like that than I care to remember, where I hung on by threads of sanity. No one knew what was happening at home. There was no one I could confide in, nor did I want to, for fear of the judgment and ramification of such. Every day consisted of a dialogue that kept me trapped inside with my lies and fears. I was repeating the same pattern I had survived as a child. I saw those patterns, but felt completely helpless to avoid or escape it. When I got really depressed and scared, feeling utterly helpless, the only safe place to turn was inwards. But even that place wasn't safe for me. When I looked at the girl in my mirror, she screamed silently back. Look at what you are allowing your children to witness. They see you being weak and cowering on the floor. They know you are afraid; look at the dysfunction you are causing in their lives. It's no wonder your son is in the principal's office every day. It's no wonder your son refuses to speak at school. Look at the example you are setting for your girls. They are both going to grow up, marry someone just like this, and take all the horrible abuse you are now, all because they won't know any better. *You* are destroying your children's lives and doing exactly what *your* mother did. What a waste of breath. *You* would be better off if you were not here at all. As a matter of fact, we all would be better off if we weren't here at all. Jesse can't hurt any of us anymore if we are all dead and gone.

Those thoughts plagued and tortured my soul. But then, seemingly out of nowhere, this voice inside me grew louder. I envisioned another, more confident version of myself. Some people have an inner badass or a goddess. I had a smart-ass, sarcastic, radical truth-teller with the ability to extract the obvious. I jokingly called her my "Chickie at the desk." She owned her shit and made lists of all the things that needed to shape up or ship out. I started asking questions of that part of myself more and more. I don't remember having an imaginary friend as a child, and I thought it was crazy to be having all these inner dialogues with myself. So I imagined a stronger, more vibrant, and radically honest version of myself who kicked her feet up on my desk, kept track of everything that was going on, and helped keep me sane. She was who I saw in the mirror, but I felt like I couldn't fully connect with her. She had the confidence to ask, "So what are you going to do about this?" She was me, but I wasn't ready to accept that truth yet. She made herself at home and began renovating my soul!

Who the hell was this girl and why was she sitting in my spot, filing my life papers, trying to dictate what should be? Had I truly flipped my wig? Was this the exact moment my personalities decided to split and greet one another? I can't answer that for sure, but there was a distinct difference between the Chickie sitting in my chair and the girl daydreaming about not getting out of the van with all five kids to walk into whatever shit-storm was waiting inside that house. I would daydream a lot about how different it was supposed to be, how much better it might be someday when he stops drinking, stops hurting himself and all of us. I dreamed about someday when we would be the amazing, happy family we were "supposed to be."

Not all my daydreams landed in such a morbid spot, but when they did, that's usually right around where I would snap back to my senses. That Chickie sitting at my mind's desk would mentally smack me in the back of the head for thinking such a thought in the first place. She would then go on a long diatribe of just how awesome life truly was, reminding me to be grateful for these amazing children and the opportunity to be their momma, and how I was serving a purpose; I just didn't know what it was quite yet. I was truly grateful. I had a job that I liked, working with people who I loved. I was sharing moments with friends safely within the confines of those walls and the playground at Sandia Learning Center. I was pursuing my education again after giving up. I was a momma to five beauties. I belonged by legal bond and marriage to a family that I didn't have to worry about being kicked out of for once! I was grateful for my growing education, as I used it to protect myself.

Even still, I used every single piece of justification I could find to support why I was staying in an abusive and dysfunctional relationship. I used my college studies to find all the viable options to offer Jesse to get sober. "It's normal to feel this lost when experiencing high levels of stress and trauma," said one research paper. "…[D]omestic violence within the home increases during pregnancies," said another research paper. "Antabuse is a medication that induces adverse reaction when alcohol is ingested," said yet another piece of research. Blah, blah, blah. I used my coursework as therapy but never reached catharsis. I separated myself from my pain.

The Chickie at my own mental health desk disagreed with me at every pass. She knew what I was doing. All those years I had been majoring in psychology and minoring in bag-packing. Thus, she understood the feelings of separation and the dire need to feel whole.

I was emotionally numb to it all. I was teaching my children to close themselves off emotionally and disconnect from reality through my own reactive behaviors. The entire time, I waited for the day I could undo it and make things grow from there. I was teaching my children, "I have to wait to live a better life."

That is another lie we tell ourselves in this life. That is out and out horse shit! I believed that at one point, and if you are where I once was, I get it. Everything around you reinforces that belief. Your family, friends, school, work schedule, weight, time constraints, money, age of your kids, rocky marriage, or maybe the circus is in town; you name it. I know you have something in your life that you're claiming is the reason why you can't live out of a positive and abundant mindset. I also know (and can promise you with evidence) that if you unpack that lie, you will live more!

Where was I? I was going to college part-time, and those courses kept me from falling off the brink of insanity. When I sat in the classrooms surrounded by like-minded people, even though I was the "nontraditional" older student, I still felt welcomed, challenged, and alive again. I felt happiness as the knowledge poured into my brain, and I was then armed to take on the world. I would leave the rooms with confidence and my chin held high with esteem again only to have it knocked out of me, literally.

Back on the plane, I was jarred out of my reverie as Justin leapt up and down on my knees now. My window of opportunity for getting him to sit in the car-seat that I had lugged down the narrow aisle of that plane was closing rapidly. My kingdom for a dose of Benadryl. He laughed and giggled and brought me out of my funk and into the present again. I remembered that I was just hours away from starting this seemingly new chapter in my life. I was ready to turn the page, even though I knew it would leave Jesse out of the rest of our story. I was ready to write his character out of the story.

As I sat there waiting, I remembered truly not comprehending why he would ever kick me in my back of all places, knowing it was the weakest, most painful part of my entire body, on a daily basis. Even years after my accident and all the physical therapy that I detested going to, it still ached all the time. I couldn't wrap my brain around why his hands were ever at my throat or why I would be on my knees begging him to stop. I would look into his eyes for any sense of recognition that he saw me, the person he loved, but it was never there. It was always as if he disappeared inside and couldn't stop the madness. I knew he wouldn't remember the fight. I knew I would wake with bruises and he would look at me and ask how they got there. We would talk again about what the last thing he remembered was and he would again apologize and beg me not to argue with him while he was drunk.

I had yelled at him again about his drinking too much and was trying to have a civilized, adult conversation about what exactly was supposed to go on *after* we had the baby, our very first child, if he couldn't string together three damn days of sobriety. These arguments always landed him in the same defensive posturing and pissed-off relay race away from me, but I didn't know what else I was supposed to do. It made total sense to me to fight for what I wanted. Fighting with him while he was lit was my not-so-bright point, and I totally own that. I had fought my whole life for everything else and this was no different. I wanted the white picket-fence and the two little kids running around in our backyard with a golden retriever like my grandparents had, lapping licks across their faces. I wanted the smell of burgers trailing across the noses of all our friends we had over to celebrate the boys' birthdays. I wanted so bad to live a life with joy, connection, and some kind of continuity.

My white picket fence was chain-link. My two boys were eleven months apart because breastfeeding is not an effective method of birth control and I didn't know better.

My golden retriever was a black, mutt-pup named Mesa. There were no friends ever because I couldn't let anyone know what happened inside these walls that I, like my mother, kept under lock and key. There were no backyard burgers or birthday parties. There was nothing "normal." No kind gatherings where you open presents and everyone is smiling and laughing and happy to be with each other. But there were hangouts at Sandia with my teachers, as well as the owner, who became like a mother to me and the catalyst for getting the heck-outta-dodge.

Sandia Learning Center was my Middletown High School. Again, I had found a haven to create a fairytale life where I was happy, welcomed, appreciated, needed, loved, and safe, but I was still not all of me. Inside those walls I was always safe, and so were my children, but I was sustaining the separation from our reality. The disconnect from our reality grew while my family remained stagnant.

The plane started to move sideways (well, turn to the right). My heart raced from the rising fear and anxiety just as much from the excitement waiting for me on the other end of this ride. The Manzano mountain tops were beautiful from this view, too. Looking down over the trails I had walked when I first moved to Albuquerque filled me with a wistfulness for what could have been. Back then, Jesse was this new, exhilarating rush of life in my veins before the reality of his disease took away everything we dreamed. We had planned to walk the La Luz trails and sit in the ruins of the stone houses.

It was a sort of cosmic irony for me. It was on top of that mountain that I had fallen in love with him. We shared who we were, who we wanted to be, with and for each other. We talked for hours about what a great life we could have and how different it would be someday…And here I was on top of the mountain again; well, soaring thousands of feet above it at speeds I cared not to think about, holding one of my bouncing babies in my lap. This time, I was headed to fulfill my pre-destined dream, to start something different.

Justin must have felt it, too. He was calming down, and I was too, as I rested my head against the seat behind me. He rested his cute blond-mop on my chest and snuggled in, I wrapped my arms around him (and hit my elbow on his car seat), looked down at him, and whispered, "Thank you." I had been wrestling with the Chickie at my desk, Justin's car seat, our carry-on luggage, and the hope building inside my heart the whole flight. I remember trying to quiet myself while Justin slept in my arms. I prayed that I would find some semblance of congruency on this impromptu trip and that something would finally make sense. I needed strength to be there for my mom while she grieved the loss of our uncle. I needed someone to watch over the four babies I had left at home with Jesse, and I really, really needed to know why the love of my life had been brought back into my life at such an odd time. I knew my life was changing. I knew I was excited to see Heath after all these years, and I also knew I wasn't saying a single word about what my life had really been like all this time. This would be the second time I chose to lie to him and myself.

The plane finally landed. I gathered up a sleeping mess of blond curls as he continued to drool on my shoulder, put my backpack on one shoulder, the diaper bag on the other, and somehow grabbed the tip-top strap of his car seat so I could drag it thudding down the aisle. "Welcome to Baltimore International Airport. Please enjoy your stay."

Justin was still asleep in my arms as the plane skidded to a full stop with such impact that it made me extremely grateful that I was strapped into the seat. I squeezed my little blond-boy and his curls just a wee bit harder. He slept through it. (Figures!) Now to get from the very back seat of this sardine can and out so I can breathe some real air instead of the stream of forced air that beaned me in the head the whole flight. *And now we wait.* Justin began to wiggle in my arms, and thus started the mental begging. *Please just stay cool. Please want to stay in my arms. Please don't get the need to pee. Please just pretend nothing at all is happening. Please pretend Mommy is not standing up in the middle of a hundred people trapped at the back of the plane, please, and thank you!*

As I finally walked off the plane, and followed the single file line out, my bags smacked the tops of every aisle seat, and the car seat in tow hit the sides of every arm rest, I was starting to get excited again. I gently alley-ooped Justin back up on my hip with that side-upwards-swing-thrust-move that moms instinctively know how to do so well. He landed squarely where I needed. I started telling him about how cool it was going to be to see green trees and grass everywhere. I told myself the very same! I couldn't wait to crest over Braddock Mountain or South Mountain, drive Highway 70 West, and see real trees for miles.

Now, don't get me wrong. I truly loved living in Albuquerque for its own specific aesthetics, but the ABQ is rock, sand, dirt, dust, and shrubs that try to pass for trees. You usually only see the tall trees that have lived a true life in the richer areas from Paseo Del Norte to Eubank and from across the bottom of the Manzano Mountain trails to about Wyoming Boulevard and Academy Boulevard, where the Tanoan elite lived.

That area of the city became quite the inside joke later in my life. I would share it with Heath, but not for about another four months or so. I didn't know it any more than he did that day. That in a matter of hours from this spot in our time-continuums, we both would be changed forever. That he would implement a rescue mission with my brother (whom he would meet for the first time in a few days from now, before I returned to Albuquerque). That he would fly across the country, pack up a tiny U-Haul with my family's belongings, and climb the excruciatingly steep hill of helping five kids he hadn't even met yet, and a woman he loved but didn't even know. That he would then drive across the country and start over without the violence that encompassed us all, only to have his whole new world be legally remanded back to the state of New Mexico. He didn't know he was going to have to choose between his new life and his old life in just a matter of months.

Neither of us could have imagined that in just a year's time we would be living in Albuquerque together, raising my five children, with me pregnant with his first, and playing mental-anguishing rounds of a twisted version of relationship Jenga, not with simple, little wooden blocks but with what grew to be nine real, living, and breathing humans hearts.

No, as I got off the plane that night, all I could think was, *Holy wow, this is unreal. What am I doing here? Oh, God, I hope Jesse is behaving...behaving?! Really? That is the way I am going to label that fear!? That's just great. I am thousands of miles away, and I am worried my husband will misbehave like one of my children... This is stupid, I need to find my bags. No, I actually need to call and check in.* I checked my phone. Still no text. *That's probably because there's no cell service. But what if it's not? What if he is just drunk again and doesn't want to call because he knows I will know the second I hear his voice? What if nobody remembers to check on the kids while I am away...* I felt my heart rate speed up. My breath came in short bursts. *Oh, this is ridiculous. I am going to have another stupid panic attack in the middle of BWI with my three-year-old. Just like my mom.*

Suddenly, I remembered being eleven years old. I was riding in the passenger seat of my mom's Buick, and we were en route to Frederick to pick up some groceries. Panic stole in over her face as we got on the ramp on I-70. "Mom, you need to speed up," I said. But she just stared straight ahead.

In the rearview mirror, I saw a car barreling toward us. I lunged my foot on the brake so we wouldn't get slammed into. But this experience here was totally different, yet exactly the same.

I heard Justin say "Chocolate, Mommy," and it broke me free from my toilet-swirling inner dialogue. Justin and

I walked some, and of course I took him on the moving sidewalk. I felt like we were getting nowhere fast. He looked down in amazement; I looked forward so I wouldn't get dizzy or miss my step and drop the boy. I tried to settle my nerves inside. I knew that whatever was going to happen was going to happen. I couldn't do anything about it clear across the country. I put all the things in place that needed to be so the best possible options were available should I need to call in back-up. Until I knew something for sure, Jesse was sober and the kids were fine.

Living with this kind of anxiety didn't happen overnight. It developed over years of the day-in-day-out not knowing what would be the same...or who would be the same in our case. I had married Dr. Jekyll and Mr. Hyde, a.k.a Jesse and Evan Williams.

I never really knew who I would wake up to each day. I never knew when my head hit the pillows each night who would be by my side. I learned to be very much in touch with what I thought were my gut instincts. In the beginning, I felt like I was just really attuned to him and his mood. I justified inside myself that I was really so in love with him that I could read his every mood just from the tone in his voice or the orange-flavored Tic Tacs wafting from his mouth. Those gut instincts were actually the survival and defense mechanisms I learned as a child going into overdrive. I convinced myself that the key to living a happy life was to help him stop drinking all the time. I started my full-time undercover job in Operation Lose Yourself in His Addiction.

I gained many new roles through those years: bottle monitor, whiskey-flask sleuth of the year, whining wife, overextended mother hen, vomit cleaner-upper, find-the-drunk-man-in-the-bush-spotter, weightlifter, good cop, bad cop, detective, nurse, judge, jury, critic, counselor, id, ego, and superego, and priest. Keeping up with Jesse's addiction, the mood swings, the cravings, the triggers, the non-trigger-triggers, was a full-time job outside my full-time job. I just didn't see it that way, then. I saw it as what I did to help him be part of the life I was building. Sometimes I wonder if I had just walked away the very first time I went home, when my mother bought my one-way ticket away from it all, how different it would have been. I wondered if the second time I returned home was the Universe's way of opening the door for me to choose again and walk through to the opportunity.

CHAPTER 16

FIRST TIMES

You don't ever forget the first time for anything. I remember the first time I lost a tooth when I was little, and I cushioned it under my pillow for the tooth fairy. I remember the first time I fell on my face at the playground and Uncle Bob scooped me up, wiped me off, and danced with me in his arms. I remember the first time I saw my step-father pick my brother up and throw him across the kitchen, and the *thud* his little body made when he slid down the wall. I can remember the days of fights afterwards and my own little voice yelling above my mother's, demanding that she just leave him and take us away.

I remember the first time I kissed a boy. It felt like he was going to swallow my whole face, and I thought if *that* is what it feels like to kiss a boy that I was never going to do it again. I also remember shopping for my first homecoming dress with my foster mom and the smile on her face when I came out of the dressing room in the emerald green spaghetti-strapped dress. I remember giving birth to my very first child and all the amazing moments that were included in those forty-eight hours before he finally was pulled the heck out with those forceps. Every happy moment was bittersweet as I also remembered the first time Jesse hit me. It was with such force that it knocked me across the room.

I stood there dumbfounded, in shock and in total disbelief. I was bleeding from the right side of my swollen bottom lip and I held up my hands to my face, which was also swelling, trying to just wish it all away. The handprints crisscrossing the front of my neck tingled as if his hands still squeezed against it. My shirt was ripped half off my shoulder and both my knees bruised from the falling. I had tried to run out of the house before he grabbed my ponytail and the back of my shirt. I had yelled, I had cried, I had tried to reason with him. Someone had heard me and called 911 and that was why a clump of my hair lay at the officer's feet. She asked me to turn sideways so the police photographer could take that first picture—proof of what my life would look like. Jesse was in the other room explaining that it was just an argument and that he hadn't even touched me. I was in the adjacent room explaining to the officer that I had fallen and that was how I got hurt. Inside I was arguing the truth away. *If you tell her the truth, you are going to lose this baby. If you tell her what really happened, she is going to arrest you for disturbance... Why the hell didn't you just leave him alone? You don't get anywhere like that. He can't make sense of anything and you wind up hurt every damn time, Tina! When will you learn to just walk away?*

The truth was, I had made him angry somehow. I don't remember what I did to provoke him, but I already knew he was half-drunk. At any level of intoxication, his temper would get the best of him. I wasn't about to let him get worse, so I hid his beer, his wallet, and his keys. Of course, that didn't improve Jesse's temper.

Jesse was arrested for aggravated assault and battery. I pawned his guitar to make his bail, attended the court hearing where he was remanded to anger management classes for six months, as well as AA. I also had called my mom and she had agreed to buy me a ticket away from this monster before I got further trapped. It took a few more months but that awful day came. In the faux happiness, there were prenatal check-ups, heartbeat monitors, a job promotion, and a few really good days strung together between all of his drunkenness. I remember bawling my eyes out as I packed my bags after the worst fight. My brother (who had moved down there after me for a time) helped me secretly get away in the middle of the night. It was just more patterned behavior playing out in the next generation of dysfunctional characters in the story line.

That plane ride landed me in front of a very angry and disappointed mother. But even that I understood. My aunt had helped my mother to escape the violence in much the same way my brother helped me. My mother had tried in her own way for years to absolutely avoid this exact outcome, yet there I was, pregnant and alone, and beaten to a pulp. It truly looked painful for her when she hugged me hello that night. I don't know if she was actually seeing me in that moment or a distant shadow of where she once started the same exact path that led us all there to that moment.

The Chickie at the desk must have thrown a mental rock at my head and snapped me back to the task at hand, just not in enough time for me to not take that walk down memory lane. As I headed out to load Justin and my luggage into my rental car, I looked around at my vaguely familiar surroundings. A lot had changed in the years I had been gone. The airport was even bigger than it was before, which meant I would get even more lost. The years had passed, but my ability to find my way out of a bag with a map and a flashlight hadn't evolved at all. I became best friends with my GPS through it all. Justin was still tired, so he was much more pliable, even though I was handling everything one-armed. I often wondered if the kids ever laughed inside their own heads at some of the stuff I did with one hand and them on one hip. I laughed a lot at that.

As I slid in the driver's seat, it was really starting to sink in that I was here. I pulled out of the parking lot thinking, *I am glad to be here*, yet wishing I wasn't at all... *I don't want to see the look on my mom's face... I can't even imagine what she looks like now... Will I even recognize her? Will she recognize me?*

While my mom had lost a lot of weight due to Graves' disease, my weight went in the severe opposite direction. I hadn't seen her since I tried to escape Jesse after that awful fight. I had only talked to her a couple of times over the years. She had sent a Baby's First Christmas ornament for my first child, but I kept her as far away from my children's lives as she more than willingly stayed. *She was going to meet her first grandchild. Well, technically her 4th,* I thought. But she hadn't ever met any of the older ones yet, so this was the first for both of us.

I kept following the GPS directions and I started to gain my footing, slowly recognizing the signs along I-270. I remembered how long it took to get from BWI to Frederick. I didn't know how much further Hagerstown would be, though, but I knew inside I was making a pit stop first. I wanted to see Bob's house one more time, the one on Wandering Trail Drive... I wanted to smell him, see his absence for myself, feel some kind of closure. I really wanted to just put on one of his button-up shirts, even though I knew I would swim in it, or one of his sweaters. I wanted to hold one of his golf clubs and swing it again; maybe that would bring him close to me. Maybe he would sense what I was doing and make his presence known. Maybe the golf club would hit me in the head and wake me up. All of this would just be some insanely strange dream and I would wake up at home to deal with the normal crazy instead of this.

My Chickie at the desk interjected again. *Normal crazy?* I sighed to myself and kept driving, looking in the rearview to check on my midget. He was soundly sleeping again. I wondered if he had any idea what was going on. Can they sense the winds of change? Is their intuition more finely tuned at that age without all the life-strife to blind them?

Out of the corner of my eye, I saw the off-ramp sign for Falls Church Road. I had plugged Uncle Bob's address into the GPS, but I honestly didn't need it for this drive. I made it all the way to the front of his driveway by following my heart's map. It was dark and there was no light on outside, but it was almost 9:30 at night. I wasn't sure if

Terry would even answer the door. My family was much more capable at drawing lines and limits than they were at openly accepting change. I, on the other hand, truly didn't understand much of the discord between all the adults when I was a child and there was an abundance of it with them. I did understand that hurt people hurt people and that the program of pain had been handed down to me. I also understood that it was a choice to keep drawing those lines and limitations or to step outside them all and begin to live.

I loved my Uncle Bob with every fiber of my being. I stepped out of the car and stood beside it staring at the house, remembering the last Christmas party I had attended there when I was eighteen. Uncle Bob followed me out to the driveway, and my face lost all its color as he saw me put a beer to my mouth. I remembered that slow lullaby drawl. "Tina, darling, just one," he said. "You have a long drive back to school." I smiled in shock and sheepishness.

He was never ever disappointed in me, just direct and honest. Even when I was little, oh geez, was he direct back then! There was nothing confusing happening when he picked my five-year-old self up, threw me over his shoulder, and walked me out of the Fredericktown Mall. I kept running around the piano store after he told me not to. And it most certainly smarted when his giant hand found my backside like promised. That was the first and last time that ever happened! It was that kind of dependability that I needed in my life and he was always there to offer it. *And now,* I thought. *It's gone. Now, there will never be another driveway conversation, another hug with me on my tiptoes to reach his shoulders, and no more giggle inside when he says "I cain't" get to the phone instead of "I can't."* That always cracked me up.

I had called his home number after she told me the news just so I could hear his voice again. I called over and over again. She wasn't going to answer the phone anyways and I was fine with that. As I stood by my car, I thought that maybe she would answer the door, maybe she would have the common courtesy of looking his loved one in the face before shutting the door on my heart again. No such luck. She did, however, open a window. As I looked at the house, I could hear the window open and see her stick her head out. And then I heard the words, "Tina, you have to leave. I am not talking to any of you."

Why does it have to be like this? I wondered. *What in the world did you adult people do to each other that makes everyone want to run for the hills? Why is everyone so damn separated and exiled from each other? How do I stop this from happening in my own life with my own kids? "I cain't" even imagine what I would do if all my children stopped speaking to me and literally moved as far away as possible. This is not a family; this is a disaster!*

I tried to question her, but she slammed that window shut and turned the bedroom light off. I don't know if she stood there and watched me cry. I don't know if any of the neighbors wondered who the crazy girl outside her house was just standing next to an idling car with her sleeping boy inside it. I do know that it took every ounce of strength I had to drive away from that home, knowing

I wasn't going to ever see, feel, or know any of what my Uncle Bob was, ever again, and that I had to go deliver that reality to my mother, out of some loyal obligation. I wasn't going to be like what everyone else grew to be. I may have strong feelings of ill-ease towards my mother and have equally justified cause to not want anything to do with her. But you just don't treat people with complete disregard like that. It's cruel!

I eventually made my way back onto the freeway and headed for my final destination that night. I got to Exit 32B in Hagerstown and the GPS led me down the Dual Highway, a right on Robinwood Drive, past a community college (that one day would play a huge part in my life) and up a hill and down again. I made the right onto Woodbridge Drive and the next right and then slowed down to look for Quailbridge Circle, and turned right again. Then creeping, I looked on the right side of this circle for Heath's house. I pulled into the available spot. With pure excitement running through my veins, I got out of the driver's side, opened the back door, unlatched a still sleeping Justin from his car seat, and adjusted him to lean his head onto my shaking shoulder. I drew a huge breath in, walked straight towards the unlit door, and knocked. No one came to the door. I knocked twice more and then confusingly backed up to look up at the numbers. I was one off. Numbers were never my jam. I got back into the car, strapped the boy back in, reversed from the spot, pulled out, and went down a few more houses. Finally, I found it. I parked in that empty spot, got out, looked up at that front door and read the numbers. I was at the right place this time. I got Justin out of the car, walked up to that door, and raised my hand to knock.

My hand had barely grazed the fake wood when a guy I'd never seen before yanked the door open. Startled, I opened my mouth before my thoughts could process. "You're not Heath," I stammered out.

"No. I'm not," said the strange guy. "But he is." He moved aside.

And there he was. My completely unknown, un-imaginable, completely-unreal future, smiling at me ear to adorable little ear as he leaned against the wall. His eyes smiled straight through me. That was the same exact stare he gave me on the doorstep outside the Chester Brook Apartments in Middletown, right before our very first kiss.

It was like that moment in all the movies where the background fades away and all you can feel is the magic in the air the couple comes to meet for the very first time. Except this was the second time. I couldn't breathe; he looked gorgeous. He looked the same as he did when I said goodbye in the Kenny Rogers Roasters drive-thru all those years ago.

My mind flooded with thoughts. *How can he still look like this? How can those eyes still be the same after all these years? Is that my heart pounding? Why do I feel like I have ten billion butterflies kissing me everywhere? Why can't I take my eyes away from his? Does he feel this too? Am I losing my mind? Oh my God, I still love him! Is this even possible? What in the world is happening right now and why can't I move?*

My heart leaped forward, taking the rest of me with it, and I caught myself in the doorjamb. He smiled, his jaw jutting to the side just like it did in high school, and said the words that started the rest of my life over again, "You can come in."

CHAPTER 17

RIPTIDE

I walked into that door and into his life completely. We've been married for sixteen years, raising seven incredible kids together. I wish I could tell you this was the part of my story where everything got better. I wish I could say that, after removing ourselves from the abuse and violence for good, that it all became easier. But as I said in the very beginning of this all, to truly live life you have to be willing to let go of lies.

The old adage goes, "Hurt people hurt people." Well, I was a hurt person and I hurt my person. For many of our beginning years, we were in fight or flight and straight-up survival mode. We had been forced to move back to New Mexico to accommodate the court order visitation. Then we had been appointed as temporary guardians of my children when their dad was arrested for neglect and child endangerment. It took us almost two years there to get the court documents signed, releasing us from staying in New Mexico. In the midst of that chaos, Heath and I were trying to be a "normal" couple.

Our normal consisted of Heath and I sitting on one side of the baseball bleachers and my ex-husband and his family sitting on the opposite side. My kids would run back and forth reporting, "Daddy wants to keep us for the night," even though he wasn't allowed. Normal also consisted of me being on bedrest because I almost miscarried Mason (my first son with Heath) because I had insanely high blood pressure.

But even in that craziness, there were some sweet times. My favorite memory of normal was a Walmart trip that Heath took me on to get absolutely anything and everything I wanted for the nursery in our beautiful new home. I had never had a new home. I had never had many of the gifts Heath offered me. That created a huge amount of pain for me, but I didn't share that with him. I didn't feel worthy of him, his love, or the amazing gifts. From the very beginning, I fought his love and acceptance of me. I was petrified that he would one day find me out and then it would all be over.

The constant inundation of emotional dysfunction that I grew up in and then continued on with in my first marriage left me with a very cold and distant side to myself that came rearing up when I was triggered. Through my dysfunctional filter, Heath's love and acceptance of me and for me and my children triggered me. I was terrified that one day all the joy and potential would just be over, that I would have to return to the pain. My fear of trauma kept me feeling traumatized. And it kept Heath at arm's-length. It also kept my kids at a distance, as well. That is what a pain cycle does to those rolling in the riptide of it. The unhealed soul has one of the strongest undertows imaginable which is why we all understand the adage, "Hurt people hurt people." The mental comprehension of that concept does not protect the self from experiencing it though nor does it save the people around you trying to love you.

I didn't mean to push him away. I didn't mean to dismiss his love, his willingness to hold space for me, or the literal hand he would hold out to me most days. I was scared. Every day was a struggle for me to move through and pretend to be fine. Looking back is always 20/20. We know that. It is what we derive from looking back and how we use it to change our story moving forward that matters most. Our significance is found in the release of what we thought one day we might become.

On a daily basis, I woke up with horrible stomach cramps and excessive runs to the bathroom. I was suffering more panic attacks again. I tried to always dismiss it as nothing more than another busy morning or having too much coffee. But the racing in my mind and the feeling of being out of control was overwhelming most days. I put my focus more on the kids and what they needed from us to be OK, trying at every turn to appear happy and safe for them and for him.

One of the greatest gifts Heath gave me in the beginning was the ability to stay at home and be more involved with them. The unfortunate part to that was I had no idea how to do that. At Sandia, I had pretty much an around-the-clock support system when it came to taking care of me and my kids. I didn't have that here. I was absolutely petrified of all five of my children. My oldest at the time was eight years old and my youngest was eighteen months. I had been a parent for eight years, but not the one that got to roll on the ground and play with them. I wasn't the mom that read storybooks and sang songs to her kids every day. I wasn't even the mom at home cooking dinner or making after-school snacks. My entire identity had been swallowed and consumed by the necessity to survive yet another life I couldn't understand why I was even in it. I was the mom constantly screaming for them to behave because I didn't want to upset their dad. I was the mom that my son had to protect when Daddy was angry. I was the mom working twelve-hour days and volunteering in the daycare's kitchen so they could stay longer and have dinner there because it wasn't safe to go home.

I was the mom filing for food stamps and waiting for midnight to hit so I could do my grocery shopping on the fifth of every month. I was the mom that had to make sure that I pulled out all the cash assistance from the ATM before their dad could drink that month's rent. I was the mom that used to go to the Phillips 66 gas station bathroom and steal the giant roll of toilet paper to save us money for food, diapers, formula, and gas.

I was the mom that sent her two oldest boys to stay at their grandmother's because the electricity had been cut off and we didn't have any money to turn it back on for at least a week. I was the mom that came home from work one night and found her three-week-old daughter strapped in the carrier and her two older brothers standing watch over her as she wailed. One boy was rocking her, and the other boy was trying to get her to take the bottle.

And yet here I was, years later, safe and loved for the first time in my life, standing in a brand-new home with the best friend I've ever had in my entire life, who this time was now my husband and step-father to my children, and it felt like I just couldn't figure out how to live this life with him.

It wasn't that I couldn't figure out how to live life with him; it was that I didn't want to accept myself, let go of my old identity, and grow forward into the sun. I needed the obstacles and pain in my life to know who I was and how to react. The truth is, we don't really want the blocks, obstacles, closed doors, people, or ourselves out of the way because that means we have to own them and let go of them. That would also mean we have control over our own lives and how and why we live them. I struggled with this reality for years. There came a point I had to start looking at which obstacles I was allowing into my life and why.

The obstacles, big or small, present or past, take up precious space inside of our hearts, our bodies, our minds—our lives and those lives you hold close. We all have them. How we respond to them and what we identify them to be are the variants. That's what makes the difference between us living a *Groundhog Day* life or living an extraordinary one where we are fully present. What we do with them, or better yet, how we perceive them is what generates the change. So I started to wonder, *how can I stop letting the obstacles have control over my life and instead use them as opportunities to grow?*

When I asked myself that question, I was astonished by my answer. I had actually been afraid of the sun my entire life because it had always been out of my reach. I had been raised to stay away from it. I grew to believe it was for others, never for me. I didn't know how to stand in it. My husband did. My children flocked towards it. I loved looking at it from afar. But I truly didn't believe that I deserved to stand in it with anyone. So, I started looking at my obstacles differently.

Obstacles are seeds planted in the garden of our lives. You are the gardener. What do you want to grow? You get to choose what you want to see in your garden. Do you want to see vibrant, beautiful life? Or do you want to remain in your lies and misery? One choice will snuff out all the life around it, and the other will grow tall and strong, bringing you abundance and joy. If we take these seeds and nurture them and treat them like they can amount to something, they will thrive. Our job then becomes identifying the weeds that could potentially snuff out our life so these obstacles can be released and serve a purpose.

There are other factors you can control to bring your garden to fruition. How we arrange the crops in the garden, the amount of sunlight the crops take in, how often the garden is weeded and cared for, these are all things that manifest growth in the seeds in our lives. The people in our lives are like plant food. While everyone is on their own separate journey, you want to surround yourself with people who will help support you on yours. You are responsible for aligning yourself with good people. When I look at the people I have grown with in my garden, I have to own that many from my past were like parasitic weeds. Not all of them were thriving towards the sun, and they were bringing me down, too.

When I started to really prune my garden, I had to step back and notice that it was overflowing with dead patches. Weeds entangled each other so thick that I could barely see the sunlight from beneath them. I was heavy with their weight and slowly suffocating in their hold.

I tried to reach for the sunshine and to purposefully plant seeds in my life. I kept reaching for the ways, trying to avoid the lies. But the pain I carried inside of me and kept buried in the soil became my own strand of strangleweed. The problem with strangleweed is that it saps the nutrients from the healthy seeds, and they can't flourish.

When I remarried, my husband and children became those incredible healthy new seeds in my garden. But because I was stuck emotionally, I started to suck the life from them. I had become the strangleweed in my own garden, swallowing up the sunlight we all needed to grow. I couldn't breathe in my own life anymore, and I blamed everyone around me. There I was surrounded by nine people and feeling utterly alone. I had run out of life-support because I didn't take care of and own my life.

Heath tried for years to replant me in his garden with our children over and over again. He met every fear that I had with love and acceptance. He held me through the emotional disorientation and through every nightmare, memory, and flashback. When I couldn't handle being touched, he gave me space. When I grew angry because he wasn't being affectionate, he held me. When he saw that every weekend ended in tears because stringing together five days was about all I could handle before breaking down, he started keeping a roll of Charmin Ultra Soft in his nightstand for me.

I had to finally acknowledge to myself that not being OK was OK. It wasn't the end game. It was actually the beginning.

CHAPTER 18

FACE TO FACE

It was time to find out exactly who I was after over thirty years of avoiding self-discovery. I started what I thought was just a health journey. It became the journey back to who I was as a woman and who I choose to be as Heath's wife, my kids' mother, and a coach and friend to you. The start of my FitMinded Living adventure uncovered the other aspects of me that were eager to live, much like the ten-year-old I had left in charge all those years ago. This entire story has been a focused attempt to release the Chickie at the desk and honor her. When we follow our truth and passion in this life, we shine the light on a path for ourselves to keep going and for others to see where to go next.

There are numerous how-to books, lists, guides, YouTube videos, apps, and gurus out there all claiming to have the answer. I read them. I listened to them. I downloaded them. I've borrowed them. I did the same thing with the how-to crap that I did with the endless array of quick-fix diet options that I sought refuge in to make my life better. Seeing that same pattern play out again stopped me in my tracks, and I hope it stops you. We don't ever again have to reach outside of ourselves for validation that we are significant.

Your mind and body, your entire life, are full of exactly what you fill it with. I found that out along the way to losing over one hundred pounds. There is something to be said about what we hold onto. Whether it's trauma from the past or "fat clothes," we clutch these things to make sure we don't get caught off-guard. I didn't want to throw out my old clothes for fear that I would have nothing to fall back on when I gained my weight back. That realization hurt. My lie with my health was that I was incapable of maintaining it, and that I would inevitably give up on being worthy of a healthy mind and body.

That lie was uncovered quite literally when Heath dragged me to a Lane Bryant outlet store to get clothes because mine were swimming on me. I had been a size 12 for well over a year by that time, but I still wore all my "heavier clothes," as well as a heavier mindset. I was petrified to let go of my fat clothes because I needed a backup plan. I was holding onto them so I would be safe if I failed to keep the weight off.

When he handed me three shirts that were all size medium, I laughed at him and straight-up said, "Those aren't going to fit me." He still encouraged me to try them on, and I begrudgingly took them to the dressing room.

I ripped the shirts off the hangers and picked one up blindly. I threw it over my head and shimmied it into place, keeping my eyes closed. If I opened my eyes and it fit, it wasn't about him being right and me being wrong about the size. If it fit, then I was going to have to see the new girl staring back at me from the mirror. I was going to have to embrace her and fully be her and I didn't know who the fuck that was. I had no concept of what my body looked like because I wasn't looking at my body through a healthy mindset. I was looking at it from a fear-based one and waiting for the other shoe to drop (a.k.a. waiting for the pounds to roll right back on). Again, I had reached another point in my life where I was existing on the surface and choosing not to live.

I was completely missing the fact that I was doing it. I was stronger, leaner, sexier, and happier. I was the missing piece in my life. In the mirror that day, I saw the hard-won body of a woman who changed her mind and started to believe in herself. I recognized the woman who still held onto fear that this wasn't real and frantically wanted to run back to what she knew, to what was comfortable. At one time in my life, it was about running back to the family that raised me and abused me because the pain was comfortable. At another point in my life, it was my frantic need to feel pain because it was the only thing I understood. This time, what fueled my journey was my self-sabotaging need to fail in order to recognize myself. It was in this moment that I remembered the old adage: You can take the woman out of the country, but you can't take the country out of the woman. I had taken myself out of the abuses at home, but found myself searching for what I had left. I had taken myself out of the abuse with my ex-husband and yet I sought to feel the perceived comforts of pain by inflicting it upon my own body.

And finally, I had taken the fat off my body, heart, soul, and brain, but they were still saturated in it and all of its crispy, crippling side effects. Another lie sat in the background: I could keep changing my body and it would look as different as I wanted it to, but if I didn't start taking care of my mind in the same manner, I was going to self-sabotage my way back to the miserable place I started from—leaving me again to play the victim. I had to start seeing the woman in the mirror that truly existed and wanted to live.

There in the mirror that day I took the proverbial really long look and what I saw brought tears to my soul. Standing tall and proud, accomplished, and happy about it, a woman who had finally transformed her body stared back at me, and now she wanted more. I was happily breaking up with yet another lie. In doing so, I saw that I needed to feed my mind to grow it the same way I learned to fuel my body so it could effectively move. I craved living. I wanted to venture out of my comfort zone!

There was so much changing outside of me and now inside, too. There, in that moment, I had come face-to-face with myself. I could no longer unknow what I had figured out. There was no returning it to the box. I wasn't just putting the lies behind me; I was releasing them from myself and my mindset. I was letting go of the weight in all its forms for good.

From that moment, I continued to pursue my own growth. I grew by investing the time and energy in myself first, and then in those I love. I had it backwards for more years than I can count. I took all the lessons I've learned along the way and realized that they happened *for* me, not *to* me. The mindset I operate from today is one of tenacity and triumph. My Chickie at the desk is a Badass, and when she raises her voice, I know it's because I am feeling silent or out of control in my life. So I pause in those moments to honor her. I allow the feelings and then release them. Learning to allow them to fluidly pass gives us a vibrant life with very little baggage to unpack.

CHAPTER 19

YOUR BEGINNING

It's your turn to pick up the pen and start writing the rest of your story. I encourage you to unpack your bag today. You've spent the last 100-plus pages learning about some of what I would've once called my obstacles or deepest darkest secrets, and today you now know how and why I see all of it as opportunities that happened for me. I am grateful that they all happened, and I'm genuinely excited that they might be one of the reasons you start to see how incredible and badass you truly are every day! I don't know you personally, or maybe I do. Either way, I want you to know now what took me years to find for myself.

You already have everything you need to live your best life. You have the tools. You have the skillset. You have all the knowledge. The only thing standing between you and the life you are ready to live is *you*. Open your bags and look for the lies you still believe. Look for the ones I shared and for ones you know have been in your bag for way too long. Once you let it go and release it from your life, you will feel lighter. The weight will come off. The angst will fade from your heart. Your mind will grow. The life you live will be completely yours.

It is your time to truly be in your power house. This entire journey I have shared with you has been my lifelong adventure to learning how to be me, unapologetically and wholeheartedly. That has taken time as you have seen. It has also taken decisions which you have been witness to the figuring out of through each moment. I have come up with a few exercises over the years to help make this transformation a simpler process to implement. You can experience the 365 Day Transformation Guide by connecting with me via email at FitMindedLiving@gmail.com and put "Power House" in the subject line to get your access pass.

We made it! I wrote my first book. And you read it. Thank you! I don't have a fancy way to end this first one, but in closing, I want you to always remember this:

We change. We are human beings. We are not fixed in place forever. We grow, evolve, stretch, lean, and rise. Now go do it all! Live, love, and learn as much as possible in this amazing life you are here to enjoy and adventure through. My friend, the Badass in me honors the Badass in you!

ABOUT THE AUTHOR

Tina Fraley is the owner of Power House Studio, a nutrition coach, certified personal trainer, and a master's level community counselor with over 20 years of experience in the mental health field. As the founder of her own business, FitMinded Living, she has developed a proven approach to teaching the tools for easier life integration and has helped thousands of men and women build a healthier, healing, and happy life.

As a mom of seven, a domestic abuse survivor, and someone that has lost over 150 pounds, Tina has embarked on her own transformational journey that taught her the fundamentals of building a roadmap to long term success by bridging the gap between the physical and emotional challenges.

In 2019, Tina developed Your Power House Online, a Virtual Boutique Gym and Well-Being Studio that offers immediate tools of transformation straight into the homes of members equipped with a team of certified trainers to guide them through the programs, workshops, meet-ups, private group trainings, and health-bet challenges. Power House delivers monthly digital toolkits—to encourage and empower the walk of well-being through all aspects of health. It is personal training for the mind, body, and life of each individual. She also became a founding member of the High Achievers Mastermind, a support group established to conquer the teachings of the High Performance Academy, a coaching platform made famous by Brendon Burchard.

Tina is very involved in her local community in Hagerstown, Maryland where she is a graduate of Leadership Washington County Class 34. She serves on the board of the Washington County Women's Commission as the president and is the vice president on the board of directors at Rise Up Hagerstown, a non-profit organization that educates and trains individuals trying to re-enter the workforce after trauma, substance abuse, and/or prison release. She is also an educator at Hagerstown Community College, teaching her six-week course on FitMinded Living, and is a regular contributor to Sass Magazine. Tina is the creator of the Women's Growth Summit, an annual conference that connects thriving women and curates their life-learned tools and resources for transformation in a day-long event that celebrates and empowers empowered women.

CONNECT

If you would like to step in to Your Power House and join the community of like-minded Badasses, you can find us on Facebook or Instagram, or simply go to www. FitMindedLiving.com and click on "Power House." For more support, motivation, and updates in an ever-evolving life of this one woman and a tribe seeking to grow, serve, and live the best life, tune into the Badass Rising podcast.

facebook.com/tina.fraley

facebook.com/groups/powerhousestudio

instagram.com/fitminded_living

eGenco

Generation Culture Transformation
Specializing in publishing for generation culture change

Visit us Online at:
www.egen.co

Email us at:
info@egen.co

 facebook.com/egenbooks

 youtube.com/egenpub

 pinterest.com/eGenDMP

 instagram.com/egen.co